SARAH MAE
AND HER KINFOLK

Lillenas Drama

SARAH MAE
AND HER KINFOLK

Monologues and Dialogues with a Mountain Point of View

by Gail Blanton

Lillenas PUBLISHING COMPANY
KANSAS CITY, MO 64141

❖ **NOTE: New photocopy policy effective January 1, 1999.** ❖

The purchase of this book entitles the purchaser the right to make photocopies of this material for use in a church or a nonprofit organization. Sharing of the material in this book with other churches or organizations not owned or controlled by the original purchaser is prohibited. The contents of this book may not be reproduced in any other form without written permission from the publisher. Please include the copyright statement on each copy made.

Sarah Mae and Her Kinfolk
Copyright © 1997 by Gail Blanton
All print rights administered by Lillenas Publishing Co. All rights reserved.

Printed in the United States.

Please Read Carefully: This is copyrighted material. It is illegal to copy this material by any means except under the conditions listed below. Amateur performance rights are granted when two copies of this book are purchased. You may duplicate individual sketch scripts from this book for $1.00 per copy with a maximum payment per individual sketch of $10.00.

Please mail your request, payment, and information to:
Lillenas Publishing Company
Drama Permission Desk
P.O. Box 419527
Kansas City, MO 64141
phone: 816-931-1900; fax: 816-753-4071
E-mail: drama@lillenas.com

Information: Title, source, and author(s) of script(s)

Cover art and design by Keith Alexander

In loving memory of my daddy

SILAS TALMADGE McCOIG

An unshakable believer in the good . . .

The good old days
good old music
good old knobs and mountains
good old Tennessee spring water
good old grapevine swings
good old rabbit and squirrel suppers
good old family
good old storytelling and history
and
good old-time religion.

CONTENTS

Preface 9

Acknowledgments 11

A Word About Dialect 13

Costumes 15

Spare Time (7 minutes)* 17

Sarah Mae's Harvest (10 minutes) 20

Empty Places (8 minutes) 23

Forgiving Charlie (12 minutes) 28

Lawrence of Asheville (9 minutes) 32

Jed (3 minutes) 35

Burning Judgment (9 minutes) 36

A Man like That (7 minutes) 42

Love Me, Love My Child (8 minutes) 46

Lord Have Mercy (6 minutes) 51

Tadge (6 minutes) 55

George (5 minutes) 57

Dovey (9 minutes) 59

Door to Heaven (7 minutes) 62

Cities, Kings, Weeping, and Things (6 minutes) 66

Mysterious Year (10 minutes) 69

Alice (5 minutes) 72

Family Reunion (one act; 1 hour, 30 minutes, with suggested music) 74

Appendix
    Family Tree 97
    Suggested Songs 99

Glossary 100

*All running times are approximate.

Preface

This book was written in response to the many requests for additional dramatic material for the character in "Sarah Mae's Offering," a monologue in the book . . . *And the Race Goes On* (Lillenas, MP-637). Please refer to it for the vital parts of her personality, mannerisms, and history, and for the flavor and appearance of her locale.

Paul Miller requested that I include some other characters so that a broader range of people could use the material. Therefore, I have created a family tree for Sarah Mae and included pieces for many of them, as well as new monologues for her. I have tried to include enough information in each of her monologues so that it is not necessary for the audience to have seen the first one, but the final call on this will have to be up to the actor or director.

The locale of this family, unless otherwise indicated, is the mountains near Sevierville, Tennessee. Sarah Mae and her brother, George, live on Old English Mountain in the most distant house up the mountain. Yet, this is not the mountaintop, where there is a huge, protruding boulder named Auger Rock. Others live farther down or scattered about the close mountains and hollows. There is no electricity, running water, and so forth. The gravel road ends at the schoolhouse/church, well below any of the houses.

The time frame for the entire book is from the early 1900s to the mid-1940s. Some pieces are dated by year; others are less specific as to time and only indicate whether they are before or after the reunion piece mentioned below.

The longest work is called "Family Reunion" and incorporates most of the characters. It is an excellent opportunity for people of all ages to work together and also includes some singers and optional musicians. Although it can stand on its own, many of its lines refer to events or characteristics that have been established in other pieces that make up this book. For that reason it might be more enjoyable to present some of the shorter things in a series, ending with the reunion. Or consider a dinner theatre in which the shorter pieces are the first act and the reunion the second act. (Please note, however, that some sketches occur after the reunion and should be used at other times.)

"At Home in the Web of Life," a pastoral message from the Appalachian Catholic Bishop, states:

> To dwell within these mountains is to experience, in their height, God's majesty; in their weight, God's strength; in their hollows, God's embrace; in their waters, God's cleansing; in their haze, God's mystery. These mountains are truly a holy place.

My prayer is that the presentation of these fictitious characters who inhabit those mountains will reflect all of these things, as well as pay respect to the simple beauty and deep wisdom of their culture.

Acknowledgments

MANY THANKS:
- To all my faithful prayer partners and encouragers
- To my sister and brothers Marjorie McCoig Whitesides, Barry McCoig, and John McCoig (1925-95) for their help in recalling many memories
- To Ralph Whitesides for the idea in "Empty Places"
- To each of several actresses who has gone to the trouble to contact me to say that she is indeed Sarah Mae; and I send each of them a whoop and a slap on my thighs

A Word About Dialect

I have incorporated some common usage and pronunciations within the text itself. To render it completely in dialect, however, would make it difficult to read and in some cases impossible to decipher the meaning. For that reason a glossary of words is included, with the pronunciation commonly used in the area. This glossary is not meant to be complete but to give examples so that the actor can develop a pattern of speech characteristic of the area.

In general, this pattern takes the easy way of pronunciation, preferring things that roll smoothly and easily off the tongue rather than sharp, crisp, distinct sounds that require more varied mouth and tongue positions. Thus the *g* is dropped from *ing; ia* becomes *y* (ammonia = amony); *o* is dropped from *to; scared* becomes *skeered;* and *Sarah* becomes *Serry*—because it takes more effort to form an *a*.

H is dropped from *him* and *th* from *them,* and so forth, when used in combination with another word. For instance, I would indicate someone by saying *him* but would say, "I told 'im."

Even though words are sometimes made a syllable longer by the drawl (bed = beh-ud; Bill = Bee-ul), generally things are shortened. Two words are better than four (i.e., "get out of there" becomes "Gow thair"). Verbs or parts thereof are often omitted altogether: "They are going to town" becomes "They going to town." "Are you asking to get chosen?" becomes "Y' askin' t'git chose?"

Some words are lengthened, though: *his* becomes *his'n; if, iffen; it, hit; once, once't;* and some words have an *a* placed before them—*a'talkin'*.

Incorrect tenses and pronouns are common, as are double negatives. This could be because at that time people here attended school a minimum of years and had more to learn in a short time, and most of it more practical than grammar. The characters should never be portrayed as dumb. On the contrary, most continued to add to their "book learnin'" with self-education by reading anything they could get their hands on, through oral history, and through apprenticeships. Remarkably, some even taught themselves a viable trade solely from reading books on the subject.

There is a particular problem with the long *i,* almost becoming *ah*—but not quite. The short *i* is often a substitute for *u* (e.g., *just* becomes *jist*) or for *e (get* becomes *git)*.

A as in *mall* becomes *aw*. *Y* is substituted for more troublesome endings—*Carolina, Caruliny; Barbara, Barbrey; tomorrow, tomorry; idea, idy.*

Then there are words, phrases, or constructions that are just part of the idiom of the culture: "The man, he went and killed the hog." "He took and kilt it." These two sentences are also good examples of the fact that words are sometimes said differently depending on the structure or the person: one said "killed" and one "kilt"; the latter did not add "h" to "it."

Some language is strangely poetic and seems out of place until their Elizabethan ancestors are considered:

commence

recollect

directly (denoting time), although it sometimes comes out *t'reckly* or *dreckly* and means "in a little while" rather than "immediately"

conceive (At least two people wanted me to remove this word from "Sarah Mae's Offering" as inappropriate for her vocabulary, but I know firsthand it would have been a common word for her.)

With these generalities stated, a limited glossary of specific terms may be found at the back of this collection.

Costumes

Refer to the family tree page to determine if characters live in the mountains or in the city. City characters should dress in casual clothes appropriate for the year the sketch indicates. No females of this era would likely wear slacks.

Mountain people dress in simple work clothes. The men can have overalls or pants and suspenders. Women need dresses, rather plain, and most of the time an apron. Both genders are barefoot a lot, but when shoes are worn both males and females wear sturdy, lace-up hightops.

If the script indicates a Sunday meeting, women might wear a blouse with some lace at the collar with a long skirt, or a fancier dress. Men need pants and a white shirt fitting high around the neck, and a tie formed by a short piece of cloth around the collar, with one end loosely looped over the other in front. Some men may also wear suits, with the jacket buttoning higher than modern suits.

Mountain men may be clean-shaven or wear beards, which they would probably not groom very often. A majority of mountain women wore their hair in a rather severe manner, usually pulled up in a bun, braided, or long and straight. They might wear combs in it also, and on Sunday would have fancier combs and sometimes hats.

SPARE TIME

Character:
OLIVIA DIXON: *neighbor of Will McCoy's mother*

Setting:
A mountain woman sitting on her porch. She peels potatoes or apples or shells peas, and so forth, as she talks. Use appropriate mountain speech patterns (e.g., *git* for *get, set* for *sit,* dropping the last letter in *ing*). Imaginary parson approaches.

Time:
Mid-1800s

Props:
Bowl with vegetables or fruit to peel
Knife
OR:
Beans to string and break; peas to shell

Howdy, Parson. Come on up and set a spell. Right there. *(Indicates an imaginary chair somewhere DS of her, so that her face is toward the audience as she speaks to him.)* Well, Parson, I'm mighty glad you come by to let me know you're gonna hold a service this Sabbath. With you ridin' the circuit, that only puts us havin' a meetin' ever three weeks. Makes it kinda hard to keep up with. I say to myself, "Is this the week or ain't it?" One week's just like any other week to me. Makes it hard.

No, I didn't say I'd be there, now did I? Well, it depends. Parson, you got any idea [pronounced *idy*] how tired I am? How it feels when there ain't never a time when you ain't tired? You know how much has gotta be done to keep a family goin', even on Sunday? Time I finish my have-tos, there ain't much spare time left for want-tos.

Don't I know the Sabbath's holy, now? This is Olivia Dixon you're talkin' to, not some heathen. Seems to me like people and animals still need feedin', holy or not. And sick folk still need tendin'. Wood's got to be brought in and water's got to be drawed. Time I'm done I ain't gonna want to walk no mile with whalebone cinched around my waist. Even if I know I oughter go. What? Do it Saturday, my eye! 'Cause, I probably won't have time to do it Saturday. It's hog-killin' day and I got to work up the meat.

You needn't get feisty with me—I'm tryin' to agree with you, if you'd listen 'stead of lookin' off in the distance some'urs and sayin', "Uh-huh" before I ever finish my sentence. I'm sayin' that sure, it'd be nice if Sunday could be a day of rest and worship. Be mighty nice for everyone concerned. Parson, I've thought on it right smart while I was ironin' or darnin' or somethin'. You know what I'd do if I was God? I'd fix it where it would be a little bit easier to live. That way folk wouldn't be so tired and there would be more time to worship. Take, for instance, what if food growed right there on the shelves of McDougal's Store? No plowin', no hoein', no weedin'. Just pick it up, take it home, and cook it.

I know, Parson! I told you I ain't a heathen. I remember when Adam and Eve sinned, God said they would have to toil over the ground and wrestle [pronounced *rassle*] with weeds. But He is the God of the second chance, ain't He? Well, maybe I *am* dreamin'. Ain't you never dreamed about a better life? No? Well maybe you're too busy tryin' to fix everybody else's. But long as dreamin' don't cost nothin', what's the harm in me ponderin' ways to make it easier to go to church? Like, what if I could run me a few hollow logs from the water right through the wall into the house and just unplug it anytime I need water? Wouldn't that save a lot of time totin' water? And I'd make lamps where they didn't need to be filled or the wicks trimmed. If I was God, I'd make light inside a lamp just as natural as seeds inside a watermelon—and fire inside a stove, for that matter. Get up in the mornin' and there it would be, ready for me to cook. No choppin' wood, no haulin'. Wouldn't that be a marvel?

Mind your tongue! I'll fight the man that calls me lazy, or a backslider either. You best remember, Parson, when you're up there singin' "Are You Washed in the Blood?"—remember somebody rubbed their knuckles bloody to get your shirt nice and white and fit to wear to the house of God. Yessir, stand in that pulpit all nice and clean and fret over our spotted souls; that's fittin'. But what about if you let us file out for home past your white shirt and white teeth, and not give one care about the way we have to struggle the rest of the week? That makes you look mighty dingy behind that preacher smile. Other words, don't let him who puts on a clean shirt boast like him who takes a clean shirt off. Yeah, that's what the Good Book says, or somethin' mighty like it. You think I don't know no scripture? Well, you'll have to look it up yourself—I ain't got time. Somewhere over there around 1 or 2 Kings—Ahab, I think it was.

So anyhow, back to the dirty laundry, if I was God I'd pull me some man over in a corner and talk, private-like. I'd say, "Look here, Buddy, if you smart enough to make a still, you smart enough to make some contraption that scrubs your woman's clothes for her." Why, a body could do all manner of things in the time that would save.

Yep, it'd be nice to get all the necessities real convenient-like, so's a body would have plenty of time to sit and read the Good Book and play with her babies and ponder about things. Yessir, if I was God, I'd fix things where everybody had so much spare time that no decent person would ever miss church or prayers or devotions. Well, I ain't God, though, am I, now?

But you reckon God ever thought about them things? Say you sure [pronounced *shore*] didn't? *(Laughs)* Well, Parson, you ain't God neither. You never know what He might do, do you now? All right. Bye, Parson; thank you for stoppin'. *(Waves him off; then)* Dreamer, huh? Time my little 'uns is grown they may have all them things. That should be one blessed, holy generation. Plenty of time to get with God. Mmmm-mm. Well, these taters need cookin'; I'd better go light some wood. *Nothin'* gets done without fire, does it now?

SARAH MAE'S HARVEST

Character:
SARAH MAE

Setting:
The scene is in the eastern Tennessee mountains in the early 1900s. The audience represents the congregation of a small church. SARAH [pronounced *Serry*] MAE is dressed in a simple work dress and is barefoot. She carries an old bushel basket, perhaps three or four other baskets inside of it.

Time:
Between 1910 and 1930

Props:
One bushel basket
3 or 4 large baskets that will fit inside it

Excuse me, Preacher sir, can I say a few words, please? I'm Sarah Mae McCoy, from up on Old English, 'crost the holler there. I believe you knowed my pa? Now I know what you're thinkin'—but no sir, it really can't wait till after your sermon 'cause, well, to tell the truth, I ain't aimin' to stay for yer sermon. I'm in right smart of a hurry. Well now, I got a good reason and I'm gonna git to it directly [pronounced *t'reckly*] if you'll hear me out. Yes sir, a mighty good reason. Whew! I'm about tuckered out. I've stopped at every [pronounced *ever*] neighbor between home and here. If I could just set my baskets down here—now don't you'uns [pronounced *yens*] worry—these ain't for the offerin'. *(Whoops; slaps thighs)*

I knowed you'uns wus havin' a protracted meetin'—matter of fact, I wus over here at it last week. I heered the sermon where all the people wus dyin' from snake bites. But old Moses lifted up that pole with the bronze serpent on it and anybody that looked on it would live. You recollect, Preacher, you told us that Jesus said He wus goin' to be lifted up on the Cross in the same way and that He would draw all men unto Him. *(Whoops in joy; slaps thighs)* Excuse me, that's a habit I got from my ma, God rest her soul. I've seen my ma nurse some folks been bit by them rattlers we got hereabouts, and that pizen wus some kind of misery. Shore would have been nice if we could have just held up a pole and got 'em cured. But I reckon that's only for prophets—and saviors.

But heerin' that sermon is partly to blame for me commencin' all this—but

I'm gittin' ahead of myself. See, what I come to do is to ask you folk to cut this here meetin' short, beggin' yer pardon, Preacher, and come help [pronounced *hep*] me harvest a crop. I know the coolest part of Saturday mornin' is gone, but we got plenty of daylight left. We can tie our heads up good against the sun—'sides, I reckon it's better to work in the sun than in the rain, ain't it? *(Whoops; slaps thighs)* Well, I reckon you're wonderin' one good reason why a body would come in here and interrupt a sacred service and ask for help with harvestin' her crop. Well, here's one: It ain't my crop; and (2) it's too big for me to harvest by myself; and (3) it's gonna be plum ruint and lost if it ain't done today—shoulda been yesterday.

I see you're all as curious as crocus wonderin' whose crop I'm aimin' to harvest. Well when I tell you you're probably gonna be sorry you wondered any such [pronounced *sich*] thing. So I'm askin' you ahead of time to give a mind to yer Christian charity and remember what it says in the Good Book about the harvest stands ready, or something [pronounced *sumpin'*] like that, and we should pray for the Lord to send out workers for the harvest. Well, I'm a'prayin' for Him to send out: you! Aw now, I know He was talkin' 'bout souls, but Mr. Payne's got a soul and you might be able to git aholt of it if you help him. Now, now, afore you git all riled up any more, just [pronounced *jist*] simmer down a minute. I know Mr. Payne ain't never darkened the door of any one of our church houses. Seems like runnin' that cannin' factory takes most of his time. Well, it must take all his time 'cause he can't even give folk like us the time of day. He's biggety and all like that; that's for shore. Don't know if you heered it, but his help got plumb wore out with one or the other of his highfalutin ways and walked out of his fields. Ever last one of 'em. Ain't been back all week. And all the t'maters in and afixin' to ruin. The big factory field full of 'em. I reckon they figured if they wus gonna do without decent treatment, then the city folk could just do without canned t'maters and Mr. Payne could do without a passel of his money. Some of the hands tore down stakes as they left, for spite, and their kids tore up the scarecrow and trompled some of the vines.

Well, he's about to git what's comin' to 'im, ain't he? Serves him right for treatin' us like dirt all these years. I feel the same way about him as you do: dirty, low-down rascal. Well then, you wonder why I'm gonna help 'im, don't you? [pronounced *doan-chee*] 'Cause sometimes we gotta do things whether we want to or not, just 'cause the Lord says so. Oh . . . I didn't never tell you how the Lord said so, did I? Well looky here, I wus walkin' back from Talley's store yesterday, and when I got as far as Mr. Payne's field I sat down in the edge there to take off my shoes. I was fixin' to run out of paved road and there ain't no use eatin' up shoe leather on these mountain washouts. Truth be known, I probably wanted to sit on old Payne's property and gloat a little over his comeuppance too. I was just sittin' there restin' a spell when the wind come along and I got a whiff of that smell—sorta sweet and acid-like. Reminded me so much of my ma's t'mater patch that I got plumb weepy and commenced ponderin'. She fretted and loved on that patch like a miser with a hundred new pennies. Every last t'mater was precious. Not one was to be lost if she could help it. Whether she planted it, or Pa, or one of us kids, all that mattered was that somebody got it to harvest.

Just then I heered that wind blowin' something [pronounced *sumpun'*] in the field—flap, flap, flap. I looked up and saw it wus a piece of cloth left over from the old ragged scarecrow flappin' against the frame. And I almost wished I hadn't looked up, 'cause that frame wus in the form of a cross, standing right there in Old Man Payne's field. I thought I was gonna have a spell or something. Then the words of that text come back to me. "If I be lifted up from the earth, I will draw all men unto me." *All* men. And in my mind's eye I saw Jesus hangin' right there by the side of New Cut Road, dyin' for Mr. Payne, just like He died for me. Rich man's field or potter's field, He would have done it no matter what. It was plumb spooky. I couldn't even move for a spell. I just sat there starin', with that wind blowin' over me.

Directly it come to me what I had to do, and I had to do it tomorrow [pronounced *t'morry*] afore it's too late. I had to show Mr. Payne that a Christian acts different from other folk. Now we all know what he'd do for us if the situation [pronounced *sitchee-ation*] was backwards—he wouldn't lift his finger to do nothin'. So all you'ns that want to act like him, you can do nothin'. But if you wanna get his goozle, you can be different and go with me to help 'im.

Is anybody with me? Why, much obliged, Preacher! C'mon, time's a'wastin'. *(As she moves, others are following. They can be imaginary or real people you have planted in the audience who actually come and take a basket.)* Thatagirl, Sudie; c'mon, Talmadge . . . Annie . . . Bart. *(Whoops and slaps her thighs; turns back to audience)* Oh, and listen: if it just sticks in your craw to think about harvestin' for Mr. Payne, why just grieve the waste of that big old field. It's a regular little world of its own. The vines have grown all good and proper, and they're healthy and purty. But they've done all they can do. If you look out over the crowd of 'em, it makes you feel right sorry for 'em. Is this all there's gonna be for that little part of God's creation? Does nobody care, after they've tried so hard? There they stand, hangin' full of hopes that they're worth something to somebody. Every one of them hopes is precious. Somebody's got to get 'em to harvest. If we don't, they will have lived—and died—in vain. Much obliged, Albert. That's right, Janie, git you a basket. C'mon, hurry. *(Picks up her basket and starts off excitedly; just before she exits, she turns back with an afterthought.)*

You know what I'd like? *(Chuckles)* I'd like Mr. Payne to be pacin' back and forth on the porch of his packin' shed, plagued with worry. And us all comin' down the hill toward the shed. And when he looked up, he might not see Moses and he might not see Jesus, but he would see us with them baskets of t-maters lifted up on our shoulders, and in that lookin' he might feel somethin' drawing him to *life! (Whoops and slaps her thighs with her free hand, having lifted her basket to her shoulder when she says those words)* To the harvest, you'uns! *(Exits running)*

NOTE: Since this has happened to me in performance, I would like you to be aware of those who may come to take a basket spontaneously. If you have used imaginary helpers, of course there will be baskets left to give to those who respond. Otherwise, be ready with comments such as "You two please share a basket" or "Here, take my basket; I can use my apron-tail."

EMPTY PLACES

Characters:
    EULABELLE MCCOY
    OTHEY MCCOY

Setting:
    The stage represents the front porch of a mountain home. There is a straight chair on the porch; also two rocking chairs, one with a cane seat and one with a wood-slatted seat. There is a bucket of water and a metal dipper, either on the floor, porch rail, or a small table made from old boards held by rocks.

Time:
    Many years after the reunion dramatized in this book, when both characters are much older.

Props:
    Porch rail or small table made from old boards held up by rocks
    1 straight chair
    2 rocking chairs; 1 with cane seat, 1 with wood slatted seat
    Bucket of water
    Dipper
    Bowl with knife and fruit for peeling
    Pocketknife
    Object to whittle

(OTHEY *enters from yard, turns the rocking chairs over so that the rockers point up, and goes into the house.*)

EULABELLE (*enters from house and throws seed from the bottom of her apron into the yard*): Here, chicky, chicky, chicky. (*When she is finished she lets her apron go and turns upstage. She sees the rockers, shakes her head, and turns them upright; then exits into house.*)

(OTHEY *enters from house with a pocketknife and an object he has been whittling. Whistles as he begins to whittle; then sees chairs. Turns them back over.*)

EULABELLE (*enters from house with bowl and apples or something else to peel. She catches* OTHEY *turning the second rocker over*): Othey, why in heaven's name do you keep on turning these rockers over?

OTHEY: What do you mean, "keep on"?

EULABELLE: I seen you do it a heap of times—a hundred at least.

OTHEY: And you just now asking me about it?

EULABELLE: You do it more and more often.

OTHEY: I beg to differ with you, Eulabelle.

EULABELLE: Twice't just today.

OTHEY: 'Case it comes up a storm, they won't blow over.

EULABELLE: Storm? It's clear as a hawk's eye, Othey.

OTHEY: Well, that's the way Sam keeps theirn.

EULABELLE *(as she turns one rocker back up)*: You ain't at Sam's. *(She sits.)* 'Sides, how you 'spect to sit in them?

OTHEY *(he turns the other rocker over and sits)*: Only when nobody's sitting in them.

EULABELLE: I can't see how Irene would go to the bother.

OTHEY: Naw, it's just Sam. She grumbles about it.

EULABELLE: I reckon so. So why did you start it, after all these years?

OTHEY: What's it to you? That's just the way I like them.

EULABELLE: You didn't turn the straight chair over.

OTHEY: Well, no, I don't care about it. It just sits there. It don't do nothing.

EULABELLE: Are you addled? What you talking about, don't do nothing?

OTHEY: Move or nothing.

EULABELLE: You saying these rockers get up and walk around?

OTHEY: Nah, they just, you know, rock.

EULABELLE: 'Course they rock, Othey!

OTHEY: I mean, when nobody's in them. Just look out there and it be rocking by itself. It's bothersome purt near to goosebumps.

EULABELLE: Ah, it's just the wind.

OTHEY: Could be. But of late I can't stand to see it.

EULABELLE: You know good and well they've always done that. If there's a breeze, it's natural as breathing.

OTHEY: They ain't nothing natural about it. It's like somebody's around that you can't see. Unnatural breathing.

EULABELLE: You mean like a haint?

OTHEY: I don't know. Just somebody letting you know they're there, maybe watching you.

EULABELLE: I never knowed you was so easy spooked, Othey.

OTHEY: It ain't spooky, exactly. It's more like sad—hangs heavy on you.

EULABELLE: I don't see why you getting plumb peculiar in the middle of your years.

OTHEY: It's like somebody that wants to be with us, maybe used to be with us, but now he's gone. There's his place, and it's just empty, like he was never even here. It just tears me up.

EULABELLE: I don't see where you get that.

OTHEY: Just like the empty horse, Eulabelle.

EULABELLE: What empty horse?

OTHEY: Woman, ain't you never been to a funeral? A dead man's buddies ride to his grave on their horses and his empty horse follows them. To me, that's a more pitiful sight than the coffin.

EULABELLE: Yeah, I guess it's like Granmaw stopping the clock the minute Granpaw died.

OTHEY: Just precisely. It's like he's saying, "When you look at this clock, remember me." Or like Paw's chair still there at the kitchen table, but nobody sits there. The same with the rockers. It's like they're saying, "When I'm gone, don't forget me."

EULABELLE: Parson Stiles preached on that last Sabbath.

OTHEY: Preached on rocking chairs?

EULABELLE: No, about when Jesus said something like "Whenever you eat this bread and drink this cup, remember Me." That what you mean?

OTHEY: I reckon so.

EULABELLE: So let the rockers rock.

OTHEY: No, give them a rest.

EULABELLE: It's not a bad thing to remember the departed, Othey.

OTHEY: No, it's bad not to. That's what bothers me right smart—thinking we have to be reminded to do something that by rights should come natural.

Nobody's gonna care who sat in my rocker or who built my house or nothing. Ah, they might say, "Ol' Uncle Othey did," but it'll just be a name, blowing in the breeze.

EULABELLE: Rocking in the breeze.

OTHEY: Yeah, we just die, Eulabelle, and leave empty places and nobody knows we was even here.

EULABELLE: Well, that's the way the Good Book tells it too. "For the wind passeth over it, and it is gone; and the place thereof shall know it no more" (Psalm 103:16). *(She sets bowl of peeled fruit down on porch.)*

OTHEY: See there, Eulabelle, don't that tell you something? About how much our place matters? Like, "Don't put yourself out, 'cause nobody's gonna care anyway"?

EULABELLE: Well, it could tell you that. On t'other hand, it could tell you you better mind how you fill up your place while you're still in it—make what rocking time you got count for something beyond the grave.

OTHEY: Well, we've shore tried to do that, teaching our young'uns and helping other folk; being neighborly.

EULABELLE: Yeah, I reckon we've done tolerable well. *(Short pause)* Maybe empty places is meant to remind us they've gone on to somewhere better.

OTHEY: Could be. But they still want somebody to remember them. Even Jesus, just like you said about the Last Supper.

(Pause; only the sound of the chairs rocking can be heard.)

OTHEY: Listen; you can even hear them *(speaks to the rhythm of the rockers)*: Remem-ber; remem-ber.

EULABELLE *(rises, goes to bucket, gets a dipper of water, and sits again; as she raises the dipper to drink)*: I'll remember you, Othey. *(Hands the dipper to him)*

OTHEY *(as he drinks)*: I'll remember you, Eulabelle.

(They rock while the following poem is read by an unseen narrator, and the lights narrow toward the chairs. On the third stanza, they rise and exit. They should try to tip the chairs backward as they leave so that the empty chairs remain rocking as the lights fade and black out after the last line.)

>If stallions ride into the sunset,
>   Where do rocking chairs ride?
>Into the clock at midnight
>   Or maybe a shade this side.

The bent toward adventure has shifted
   For cowpokes, slowpokes, and such:
Bridled in legs or shoulders now—
   But bodies don't matter much.

For spirits are riding still straighter,
   Stalking a distant mirage;
Smiling, serene, together—
   The ultimate camouflage.

The riders fade into the gloaming—
   Gray stallion and spotted mare;
And the rockers into their homing—
   One slatted, one cane-bottomed chair.

FORGIVING CHARLIE

Character:
    Sarah Mae

Setting:
    Begins in the congregation and then moves to stage of the sanctuary. Represents a revival meeting in Sarah Mae's schoolhouse/church, in which the preacher has called for testimonies.

Time:
    1912

    Yessir, Preacher, if you're calling for testimonies on that subject, I think I got one. You want me to come up there or just stand here at my seat? All right, I shore will. *(Goes to stage)* We're much obliged to you for coming to preach our revival, Reverend. My name's Sarah Mae McCoy, and we're pleased to have you.
    Well, my story starts out one day in Sunday School several year ago. Some of us had got together and decided to teach a class for young'uns every Sunday—in the summer anyway—instead of just the weeks the parson could come up here to preach. Everybody enjoyed it, and it seemed like the kids was learning purty good. We was right proud of ourselves, teaching them Bible verses and making them repeat them to us straight out till they got it word for word. Way I figure it, them's rules for living and you better be right about how the rule goes, huh? *(Raises eyebrows at audiences for approval)* 'Course, it made them proud of theirselves, too, so they like it. Well, all but one or two. I scolded X. L. Bates one day for not being kind to one another after he had done learned it from Ephesians. He said he wished I would go down the mountain and sit and read my Bible in the middle of the railroad track. But most of them was a real delight. *(Emphasis on first syllable)* Things would come out of their mouths that would make me just cackle; but then I might ponder on it a minute and it would be like the sparkle in their eyes would suddenly light up the shadow over my eyes, and I could see a whole new way of looking at something. They would just say it so innocent and simple, but it was a lot more innocent and a lot less simple than they knowed, 'cause it come from something beyond them. Holy jokes, I call them. Like that something that paints a different daybreak every morning just so you can be surprised and He can laugh at your pleasure. Holy jokes. They're like holy ground, 'cause they make you stop and take notice of what might be going on, what you might learn. *(Whoops and slaps her thighs)* Them are precious times!

One day when I was trying to deal with a girl that wasn't so precious, somebody said that two kids who was visiting kin in Grapevine Holler had come in to take class that Sunday. I turned around and my heart just melted like ice in the spring. They was twins, one red-headed and one kind of strawberry blonde. Purtiest little girls you ever saw. When they smiled back at me, that spring in my heart just turned on into summer—complete with rivers swimming in my eyes and running down my cheeks. See, I couldn't think of nothing but my sister Janie's twins; and how they probably would have been just that beautiful if they had lived. And if they hadn't died, and I hadn't seen her die trying to birth them, maybe I wouldn't have been so afeared to have babies of my own. So I said they would be my special charge that day. I soon seen they was purty on the inside too—sweet and obedient. So I just took up with them, and they took to me too. I saw they met everybody and knowed where everything was. We worked together and laughed together. It was silly of me, but I started to pretend they was Janie's girls I was teaching. And before long I had become a mother and these angels was mine. When they bent their heads over to write on their slate, I took my hand and pushed them silky curls out of their face and behind their ear, and it was like a dream come true. So naturally I said I'd wait with them when everybody else went home. They said their daddy was coming to walk with them. I soon found out why he was a little late.

I was straightening up the front of the room when Faye and Mae squealed "Daddy!" and went running to the door. I turned around to go meet him, but his back was to me right then. He had one girl in each arm and they was kissing his cheeks and he was laughing. It hurt my heart some, I admit. There, standing in the doorway blocking the sun was the image of the perfect father. He told the girls to play outside and wait for him. I had thought I wanted to meet him, but when he turned to me I whirled around and closed my eyes to keep from falling. My heart was pounding like 50 pairs of feet at a barn dance. Felt like somebody was sawing a fiddle bow across the pit of my stomach too. *(Voice breaking)* It was Charlie. Charlie who left me, promising to come back soon and fetch me. Charlie who never kept that promise. Charlie who was now saying, "Hey, Sarah Mae. *(Pause)* Ain't you gonna speak to me?" I stood against the desk to steady myself, but it didn't help my voice none. "What are you doing here, Charlie?"

"I wanted to see you again, Sarah Mae. It's been a long time. How you been?"

"About 15 years," I said.

"Well, I don't blame you if you don't want to talk to me, but won't you turn around and let me look in them pretty brown eyes again?"

A little thrill went through me. I forbid it, but a thrill don't take orders. It's a shame, ain't it? So there I was turning around looking at that handsome rascal, closer than he had been a minute ago, but playing fidgety fingers around his fine-looking hat he carried. And somehow I stood there and listened to his tale, turning the colors of love and sympathy, and distrust and anger, and Maud Muller's might-have-been. How he had done well for hisself and married there in Nashville, but never stopped thinking about me, 'cause she couldn't hold a candle to me, but she would give him kids. I told him I noticed that, but it had just come to me they was seven, which meant they must have been born the same year my maw died. He seemed to have a knack for being happy when I was sad.

"Did you get back on good terms with your maw before she died?" he asked.

"Yes, I did, Charlie, which is more than I plan to do with you."

So he commenced to ask my forgiveness, to tell me how sorry he was, what a young boy he had been, what a fool he had been. "Still are, if you think I'll forgive you. And I ain't the fool that'll fall for your smooth clothes and smooth talk. Where's your wife?" I expected him to say, "Back in Nashville" so I could say, "Well, get your sorry self back to her" and then hightail it out of there. But he didn't. He said his wife died almost a year ago and he had been thinking about me a lot lately; how he had found out from the neighbors if I was married, what I was doing today, and figured out the best way to get close to me to speak his piece. Well, it almost worked, but I didn't let him know. "And you thought you could do that by using your girls to jump me like checkers on a board?"

"Yeah," he said, "I thought you might want to crown me."

"Just precisely. You gotta lot of nerve wanting me to see you had twins when you know Janie's died."

That's when he led me into temptation, but thank the Lord I got past that on into indignation. How he still loved me, how lonely he was, and how happy we could be. What a nice place he had and what purty things he could buy me. He said since I hadn't ever married I must have some feeling left for him.

"Not necessarily," I said. "It could be that I just didn't want to get hurt again." But I was fixing to. 'Cause he put on his most pitiful face while he told me I shouldn't be denied the privilege of being a mother just 'cause I was scared of birthing; and certainly his girls really needed a good mother and he was hoping I could go back with him directly 'cause they needed to be loved and cared for. "Is that so? So did I, Charlie. I needed that too!"

We went back and forth like that for a while before I got it through his noggin that I would not go back with him. Nosiree. He seemed gen-u-winely disappointed and stood there with his shoulders drooped like he had lost his best friend. That tickled me so good that I let a little smile crack my anger, but it turned back to solid anger when he said, "Well, if you won't marry me, will you at least forgive me?"

"Forgive you? Why should I? You ruined my life, you sweet-talking son of Sevier." He said after all these years he didn't want me holding no grudge. I didn't; it was holding me. Said he was a changed man and didn't want no enemies. Well, he shouldn't have been so good at making them, then.

"Sarah Mae, are you gonna stand right here in the church and tell me you won't forgive me?"

"This ain't a church; it's a schoolhouse!" He reminded me it was what we used for a church and made me say if I was a member. He had got born again and went to church regular and said he knew the right thing to do was to ask my forgiveness even if he didn't deserve it. "And now 'cause you wanna do the right thing, you want me to forget everything just like that? You don't know how people gossiped and laughed behind my back. You don't know the pain I went through waiting for you while you was happy and having a big ol' time, getting a family and moving up in the world."

"It's not exactly like that," he said. "We had two boys born dead, one just a year ago. I reckon I know what pain is. Even right now."

"Charlie, did you ever wonder where I had gone? You don't know how it was to go back to live with Maw. I was humiliated."

He just stood there and looked at me a minute real sad-like before he said, "Well, she must have forgiven *you* then. It's not a bad thing to get humbled, Sarah Mae. I thought you would have learned that by now."

He said good-bye then and held out his hand. I knowed in my soul I should take it, but I didn't do it. The girls ran in just then, grabbed my dress—one on either side—and said, "This was our teacher today, Daddy; she taught us about Jesus." I knew what he was going to say next.

"Oh, she teaches about Jesus?" I looked down at those twins and up at Charlie, then back at them and down at the floor. With a big sigh of prayer I met Charlie's gaze square and said, "I forgive you, Charlie, for His name's sake."

He smiled and nodded his head. "Say good-bye, Faye." I looked at her. "Say good-bye, Mae." I looked at her and just like that it hit me. I raised my eyebrows at Charlie. He smiled and said, "Your namesake."

I hugged all three of them good-bye! Them was holy, holy hugs, and I climbed back up to Maw's place like I was light as a bluebird feather blown along by the wind.

LAWRENCE OF ASHEVILLE

Character:
　SARAH MAE

Setting:
　Church sanctuary on a neighboring mountain; or SARAH MAE's schoolhouse/church

Time:
　Around 1931-32

　　Well, I'm much obliged to ye, Preacher, fer letting me speak about this again. And I'm plumb glad you ain't one that don't suffer women to speak in church. I know lots of yens done heard this story, but they's a tale going around that it never happened at all. That it was just a rumor—one of them tall tales that gets started for fun. So I'm pert near bound and beholden to tell it again, being's that I was there and saw it with my own eyes.

　　It was January of the year, and my brother Carmel come up from Newport. Seem like I couldn't get warm that day. The wind was cutting down through the holler like one of them whips George braids for the kids out of poplar bark. Wheeesshh, wheeesshh, wheeesshh. I went out to the creek to fetch some butter—see, we got a little place fixed in that cold water where we can keep our cool things. Ain't nobody totes ice way up on Old English where I live. Ain't no need, neither. Ye'd know that if you ever jumped under that water spout naked in the middle of July. That's about how cold I felt getting that butter. I was looking through them bare trees, and they was just going this way and that, so hard that the limbs was bumping each other with a kind of clicking sound. With the whole orchard doing that, it was a mite spooky. Sounded like they was coming to life. Reminded me of old Ezekiel and his dry bones. Made a shiver go through me that I knowed was more than the cold.

　　Sure enough, just after midday Carmel showed up, not his normal visiting hour, or even month for that matter. "Sarah," he said. He's the only one that calls my name proper. Everybody else says "Serry" like we do in these parts. He says, *(very dignified)* "Sarah." He's a preacher. *(Whoops and slaps her thighs)* Then he told me our brother over in Asheville had had a heart attack and died suddenly. They wanted him there as quick as possible, but he come by first to offer me a ride. Everybody over there was so tore up that they needed him to help make all the 'rangements, being's he was accustomed to things like that. You know, the folk in the city don't just wash 'em and lay 'em out anymore. Oh, they still put 'em to lay a corpse in the living room and sit up with the body all night. And they still carry it over to the church for the funeral. But first they gotta take it over to the funeral parlor. They're the ones who prepare the body. That's the custom now—well, more than custom, it's the law they tell me. Instead of loving, tender hands washing the body, there's needles and tubes draining and filling it with some concoction, supposedly to make it stay presentable longer. It was a good thing in this case, too, because they held off the funeral four days waiting on Carmel to get there. You see, it was snowing before we even got down to his auty-mobile. Not that we wasted any time. I put my apron up over my head and cried a spell—it was such a shock to hear about Lawrence, and think that I wouldn't never see him no more. Carmel just sat there looking solemn while I threw a few clothes out of my trunk into a tow sack. Then we lit out as fast as we could go, which turned out not to be too fast, 'cause time we got to a main road, we figured it best to go to Carmel's and hope for better weather in the morning. But it was done the third morning before folk reckoned it even possible to get over the big mountain.

We made it just in time to find them over at Lawrence's church. It was a wonder, really. We hadn't been able to reach anybody, so we figured they had already had the burial. But the family was just gathering in the back to go in. They commenced to question Carmel soon as they seen him. "What took you so long?" "We 'bout give up on you, boy." "Oh, Carmel, if you had only been here, you could have helped us make up our mind about things." "Why didn't you come sooner? We needed you something awful." Lawrence's wife just looked at us and busted into tears, and that made me start too.

"I want to see him," said Carmel. "Where is he?"

When he looked down the aisle and saw that coffin at the front already closed, he cried like a baby. Reckon he loved Lawrence a right smart. "You folk go on in," he said. "I'm not quite ready."

Our brother Tadge told him they never meant to slight him, but they had to go ahead and get somebody else. But he was sure Carmel could help preach the funeral if he wanted to. Carmel said, "No need," and motioned all of us to go in.

Somebody sung "In the Sweet Bye and Bye," and the preacher was walking to the pulpit when there was a noise at the back and Carmel come marching down that aisle like he was wearing seven-league boots. Stopped about three-quarters of the way down, everybody staring at him, and him staring at the coffin. Of a sudden he hollered, "Lawrence, come out!" Everybody looked away, a little embarrassed. Don't seem right to look on a person that's done let their grief undo their wits. So if that's what you heered about Carmel, that he stood there and hollered that, in this day and age, well it's true. That's what he done.

For a minute it was deathly quiet, like a church can be sometimes, like the whole church was a tomb. *(Long pause)* I saw the leaves move first, the ones on that big bunch of flowers they put on top. I thought it was a little draft stirred up from somebody's fan. But then it commenced to sorta bounce up a little and slid off in the floor. Huh! Put the fear of God in everybody for a second, till we realized it was just the flowers fell. Probably wern't fastened on there good. You could hear folk shift and let their breath out. And soft whispers here and there, like a little breeze giving some relief to hot grapevine leaves. Then, wham! The top half of that lid flew open and Lawrence sat up and looked at all of us like we had just brought him in to a surprise birthday party. *(Whoops and slaps her thighs)*

"Open that thing and let him get out," Carmel ordered. I don't know who did, 'cause there was a ruckus like you never seen. People running; people screaming; people crying in pure-T fright. The next thing I knowed Lawrence was swinging me around, and he threw me to Carmel and he was swinging me around, and I ain't never seen the likes of such going's on in a church and ain't likely to again, more's the pity.

Lawrence don't talk about it. Carmel neither. Not to nobody, not even me. I asked him why one time. He said, "No need."

The story got around and some folk said Carmel was a saint or prophet or something. But he weren't. Got sugar and died hisself a few years later. "Nah, he wasn't no prophet," Lawrence said. "He was just a preacher. Truth, he was taught not to waste nothing, so he just took what he had and used it." *(Whoops and slaps her thighs)* I reckon he did! Makes ye ashamed of our trifling faith, don't it? No wonder folk think it's a rumor.

JED

Character:
JED MCCOY: *Will McCoy's brother*

Setting:
Church sanctuary, testimony time

Time:
Before reunion

Wellsir, if you're asking, I figure I'm sort of like Jesus. Oh, don't get me wrong, I don't mean holy or nothing like that. I don't even compare myself to Him 'cept in this one quality maybe I figure I can identify with Him. You see, what He could do, He could walk into the Temple or the syn-e-gog or just into town—anywhere there was a bunch of people—and He could look around and study for a minute and then tell you right off the sum of how many believed Him and how many didn't. Wherever He went, didn't matter iffen they was Pharisees or teachers or disciples or just folk, He knew if they was good and sound or hollow at the core. Romans, Jews, Greeks—any kind that could be made into something, He counted in His tote.

And wellsir, you see, I'm a timber estimator. The only one for a good piece roundabout. I get called everywhere in these parts to look at stands of timber somebody's getting ready to log or sell off. See, I got this knack. I didn't learn it; it just come from the good Lord, like all knacks do, I reckon. I can look at your trees whilst I step off your land and study it for a few minutes. Then I can tell you how may board feet of good lumber you can get out of it. Don't matter if it's oak, birch, elm, pine, maple—some of it's sound and true and some of it you can't really make nothing solid out of. Some of them look just like good trees, too, but they're all bark and rotten inside, or hollow, or too soft to last. Anyway, I can look around and tell you the sum of what's real, true trees that are gonna be of some use. And I make my living helping folk out like that. Like I said, Old Jed here has the knack and I'm thinking, shucks, I might could come here on Sunday and look all around and study on it a few minutes and tell you the sum of a few things. But I don't think I would do that 'cause it might be dangerous. Jesus said that some trees weren't fit for nothing but to cast into the fire (Matthew 7:19). Still, it's something to think on, ain't it? We never know who might be looking us over, and it might be Somebody with the sure-nuff knack.

(Starts to exit; turns back) Makes you wanna grow up straight and true, don't it? *(Says while exiting)* Yep, it shore does. Straight and true. Solid to the core. Shore does.

BURNING JUDGMENT

Characters:
> Sarah Mae McCoy
> Eve McCoy
> George McCoy: *Sarah's brother*
> Talmadge McCoy: *Eve's husband and Sarah's brother*

Setting:
> Talmadge and Eve are visiting George and Sarah Mae. They are on the porch. Talmadge, Eve, and George are seated. Sarah Mae stands with a bucket of raw peanuts in the shell.

Time:
> After reunion

Props:
> Bucket of raw peanuts in the shell
> Pan of burned peanuts
> Pan of good roasted peanuts
> Porch rail or old wood table

Sarah Mae: George, I think I'll parch these peanuts for Tadge and Eve.

George: Nah, you better let me do it.

Sarah Mae: No, you go on and talk to your brother. I'll do it.

George: He's your brother too. 'Sides, I'm afraid you'll burn them up. *(Takes bucket from her)*

Sarah Mae: I ain't gonna burn them. You think I can't do nothing?

George: You have to watch them real close.

Sarah Mae: Does it look to you like anything's wrong with my eyes?

George: Now listen, Sarah Mae, this is our kin from the East. I don't want the vittles messed up.

Sarah Mae: You stubborn old man. I ain't gonna mess them up.

George: Yes you will. You'll get in a big way of talking and let them burn.

SARAH MAE: I'm afixin' to make the back of your britches burn. Now give me them peanuts.

GEORGE: Ah, all right. Don't get the oven too hot, now.

(SARAH MAE *threatens to hit him with the peanuts; then exits to kitchen.*)

GEORGE *(returns to seat)*: Stubbornnest woman I ever knowed.

EVE: It runs in y'all's family.

TALMADGE: Women don't want you fooling around in their kitchen 'less it's to wash the dishes.

EVE: We don't want you acting like we can't do nothing.

SARAH MAE *(enters)*: Especially considering all we do.

TALMADGE: What you been doing lately, Sarah Mae?

SARAH MAE: Well, let's see—got me another rattlesnake.

TALMADGE: You gonna get bit one of these days.

SARAH MAE: Me and you both if I don't keep catching them and putting them away. *(Whoops and slaps her thighs)*

GEORGE: She's got them put up in al-ke-hol in a big old glass jar.

SARAH MAE: Down in the shed with the others. Wanna see him?

TALMADGE: Well, shore.

EVE: I don't know about that.

SARAH MAE: Aw, come on, Eve. It's better than the carnival—devil in a glass jar.

EVE: I believe that.

(*They all rise and exit as the lights black out briefly to show passage of time. All reenter as the lights come back up.*)

TALMADGE: How many of them did you catch, George?

GEORGE: I dunno. About half, I reckon.

EVE: I didn't know you had so many.

TALMADGE: Tarnation, it's a regular Rattlesnake Row.

SARAH MAE: Yep. *(Whoops and slaps her thighs. Suddenly looks concerned and runs through door to the kitchen.)*

EVE: Law me, I won't sleep a wink tonight. Them snakes'll be crawling all over my bed.

GEORGE: Well, just sit up and talk all night with me and Tadge.

(SARAH MAE *enters with pan of badly burned peanuts.*)

GEORGE: You burned them peanuts!

SARAH MAE: Yep.

GEORGE: Dadburn it, woman! I told you you have to watch them.

SARAH MAE: Well, I wouldn't have forgot if we hadn't gone down to the shed. Now just leave me be.

GEORGE: You could have come back and checked them. Just carelessness, that's all it is. Ain't that right, Tadge?

TALMADGE: Aw, George, anybody might have forgot. We got to talking and—

GEORGE: That's what I told her she'd do! Ruined good peanuts. That just burns me up.

SARAH MAE: Simmer down, George. We got company.

GEORGE: Can't even do a simple thing like parch a pan of peanuts for them either.

SARAH MAE: My stars, I just showed them to you for a joke. All I got to do is put in another pan.

GEORGE: Oh no you don't. If you can't do something right the first time, don't do it at all.

SARAH MAE: Fine. Do it yourself then.

GEORGE: I shore will. And I won't make no mess like you did. *(He exits to kitchen.)*

SARAH MAE *(sets pan of burned peanuts on porch rail)*: You'd think I burned the house down. Sorry, yens.

TALMADGE: Aw, don't worry about it. He just likes to raise Cain.

EVE *(indicates* TALMADGE*)*: Runs in the family.

(SARAH MAE *whoops and slaps her thighs.*)

GEORGE *(returns)*: What you squealing about, Sissy?

SARAH MAE: Just talking about how *close* our family is.

GEORGE: You're getting next to me, that's for shore.

TALMADGE: Aw, just sit down and hold your horses, George. *(Begins to laugh softly to himself. Laughter gradually increases until everyone is looking at him.)*

EVE: What's so funny?

TALMADGE: Hold your horses. *(Still laughing)*

GEORGE: What?

TALMADGE: Remember that time we held the horse for Junior Spivey?

(GEORGE *begins laughing also.*)

SARAH MAE: Whose horse?

EVE: What kind of horse?

TALMADGE: Tennessee Shooting! *(He and GEORGE laugh harder.)*

SARAH MAE: You mean Tennessee Walking Horse?

TALMADGE: No, Shooting.

GEORGE: Actually, it was more like a birch.

SARAH MAE: A birch horse?

EVE: All right, y'all, what's the joke?

GEORGE: Junior Spivey played the joke on hisself.

TALMADGE: Yeah, he did. At school we used to play bucking bronco at recess. We'd find a short, strong sapling and bend the tip over as far as we could. One or two boys would hold the tip down while another boy got astraddle it farther back. When they let go, he held on for dear life and rode the tree till it quit swaying. Then he shinnied down.

EVE: Sounds like a bunch of boys.

SARAH MAE: Yeah, I've heard this tale before. *(She goes quietly through door to kitchen.)*

GEORGE: Old Junior wanted a better ride. He brought a rope one day and lassoed the top of a tall, skinny tree. It took six or eight of us to bend the tip over and hold it while he took the rope off and climbed on.

TALMADGE: We tried to tell him it felt mighty strong.

GEORGE: He didn't pay no mind. Said, "Let 'er rip!"

TALMADGE: That thing whipped back like Lash Larue and shot him out of there like a slingshot. *(They are laughing again.)*

(SARAH MAE *enters quietly and sets a pan of perfectly roasted peanuts on the floor out of sight. Motions to* EVE *to be quiet and takes the pan of burned peanuts inside.*)

EVE: Lawzee me, did he get hurt?

TALMADGE: Nah. Just buggered up some. Landed in a big patch of briars.

GEORGE: And 'member, Mr. Spillers came out and said, "Take up that rope and cast it in the fire!"

TALMADGE: Yeah, we was all the time laughing at him for saying, "cast" instead of "throw." "Cast it on the floor!" "Cast it out the window!"

GEORGE: I dunno, though, Junior might have got hurt some; he never did talk right after that.

TALMADGE: Shoot, he never did talk right before that.

(SARAH MAE *enters and sits.*)

GEORGE: Lord love him, what a heathen!

SARAH MAE: That's the Spiveys all right. 'Cept for Granny. She was a God-fearing woman. Writ purty poems. You writ any more poems lately, Tadge?

TALMADGE: Aw, none that's any good.

EVE: Yes you did. That one you wrote to go with your Sunday School lesson about the woman caught in adultery.

SARAH MAE: Tell it to me.

TALMADGE: Aw, that's just a little five or six line thing.

SARAH MAE: Tell it to me anyway.

TALMADGE: How come?

SARAH MAE: So's I can tell if it's any good.

TALMADGE: Oh, all right. "I squeeze my eyes shut . . ." Let's see, how did it go?

GEORGE: Because I'm a slut—

SARAH MAE: Hush up, George!

TALMADGE: I squeeze my eyes shut
    Alas, I am caught
      And I flinch at the blows to fall.
    I open my eyes
    Indeed I am caught—
      In a love that forgives me all.

SARAH MAE (*whoops and slaps her thighs*): That's fine; mighty fine. Uh, George, hadn't you better check on your peanuts?

GEORGE: Lord-a-mercy! (*Jumps up and runs inside*)

(SARAH MAE *and* EVE *try to keep a straight face.* TALMADGE *hums "Love Lifted Me."*)

GEORGE (*returns sheepishly with pan of burned peanuts*): Dog take it! I didn't think it had been that long.

SARAH MAE: What you got to say for yourself? *(Silence)* What you got to say about me? *(Silence. She retrieves pan of good peanuts and swaps with* GEORGE, *who looks bewildered. Then she says directly to audience.)* Let him who is without sin cast the first peanut!

A MAN LIKE THAT

Characters:
    LINDY MCCOY: *Sarah Mae's nephew*
    CONNIE: *Lindy's wife*
    SUSIE: *their daughter, three to five years old*
    MAN: *large, unkempt, rather wild-looking*

Setting:
    LINDY, CONNIE, and SUSIE have come from their home in a distant city to visit Sarah Mae and are on their way up the path to her home. At rise they are at extreme stage left, crossing slowly to right.

Time:
    Before reunion

Props:
    Stick resembling a snake
    Knife
    Stick to carve

CONNIE *(yelps)*: What was that?

LINDY: Just some birds in the broomstraw.

CONNIE: Not a snake?

LINDY: I don't think so. If it was, it was running the other way.

SUSIE: Where to, Daddy?

CONNIE: Why do we have to come up here anyway?

LINDY: Because I want to see Aunt Sarah Mae. She's my favorite aunt.

SUSIE: Mine too.

CONNIE: Why doesn't she move down the mountain some, where there's a road?

LINDY: Oh, she's been here too long. She loves it too much.

CONNIE: Well I just hate it: the climbing and the bugs. *(She swats at some.)* And these weeds terrify me. Look, they're higher than Susie's head. Any kind of varmint could hide in there. *(Screams and grabs* Lindy *with one arm and* Susie *with the other.)* Lindy!

Lindy: What?

Connie: What's that on the path up there?

Lindy *(walks a few steps ahead, picks up a stick and swerves it at her)*: A snake!

(Connie *screams louder.*)

Susie: Daddy!

Connie: Oh no, do you think any of those men heard me?

Lindy: What men?

Connie: You know.

Lindy: What?

Connie: Those deranged men that creep around up here. Never have been out of the mountains.

Lindy: You listen to too many tales, Connie. I doubt people up here would harm a flea. Unless they were hunting for food, of course.

Susie: We don't have any food with us.

Lindy: I didn't mean they'd hunt you, Susie. They might shoot them a squirrel or possum.

Connie: No, there's been too many stories. Some of them are bound to be true. Long, tangled-up beards and hair, filthy clothes. They say they don't like strangers messing around, and they'll make you sorry you ever set foot here.

Lindy *(laughs)*: I've set my foot in here plenty of times when I was a boy.

Connie: Wild men. Some of them raised by animals.

Lindy: Connie, stop it. You're scaring Susie.

Connie: I can't help it. I can feel them watching me.

Lindy: She's just kidding, honey.

Connie: You don't believe it?

Lindy: I'm sure there are a few who act strange. And they may hide if they hear you coming because they're not used to anybody but neighbors, and they're sort of bashful. Or they may have a still someplace and think you're a revenuer.

Connie: That doesn't say they're not mean as the devil. Doesn't take but one to kill us.

LINDY: Ah, Connie . . .

CONNIE: Are you saying it's not possible?

LINDY: Well, it's possible for a mean person to be anywhere but—

SUSIE: But not anywhere close, right, Daddy?

CONNIE: We hope not, honey, 'cause you can't trust people like that.

LINDY: People like what?

CONNIE: Sneaky. Shifty-eyed, bushy-haired. Heathens.

LINDY: That's enough, Connie! Nobody is going to bother us, Susie. *(To* CONNIE*)* You're just trying to ruin my visit because you didn't want to come.

CONNIE: I am not.

LINDY: Yes you are.

Connie: No I'm not. I want you to have a good visit.

LINDY: Then stop complaining. *(He steps carefully as onto a rock in an imaginary stream at extreme SR.)* Here, give me your hand.

CONNIE: What for?

LINDY: So I can help you across the creek.

Susie: Where's the bridge?

LINDY: They don't have a bridge. We'll step from this rock to that one, and that one, and then up on the bank. Nothing to it.

CONNIE: I'm not going across there.

LINDY: Come on; it's the only way. I'll help you.

CONNIE: I can't jump that far. Those rocks are slippery.

LINDY: I'm not going to let you fall.

CONNIE: You sure won't, 'cause I'm not coming in.

LINDY: Don't be silly. It's easy. Here, I'll take Susie first.

CONNIE: Didn't you hear me? We're not going across it.

LINDY: Connie . . .

CONNIE: No!

LINDY: OK. Fine. I'm going. You can wait for me here.

CONNIE: Fine.

(LINDY *crosses "creek" and exits right.*)

CONNIE *(shocked):* Lindy!

SUSIE: Daddy! Mommy!

CONNIE *(walks left a few steps):* It's OK, honey. He wouldn't leave us. He'll be back for us in a minute. We can—uh—look for pictures in the clouds. Look, what does that one look like?

(MAN *enters left, upstage if possible, crossing slowly down to the path, keeping his eye on* CONNIE *and* SUSIE. *He looks pretty much as* CONNIE *described. He may pause left and pick a weed to chew on, or carve a point on a stick to give time for* CONNIE*'s reaction to him.* CONNIE *grabs* SUSIE *and moves quickly to the "creek" but is afraid to cross. Makes a move toward the weeds but cannot bring herself to go through them, so they stand waiting. Their faces reflect fear, although not a melodramatic terror, as the* MAN *draws closer. They try to force bravado, but their uneasiness shows through.*)

MAN *(crosses right; when he is right at them):* God bless you, ma'am. God bless your young'un. *(He continues into the "creek," then turns.)* You'ens lost?

CONNIE: No. We're on our way to visit a relative, but I don't think we can make it across the stream.

MAN *(laughs):* This little branch? *(Comes back toward* CONNIE, *embarrassed)* Well, I reckon I could—uh—not meaning no harm, ma'am, I could—uh—carry you'ens across.

CONNIE *(not agreeable to that):* Well, I don't think—

(MAN *puts one arm around her; as he does,* LINDY *enters right.*)

LINDY: Ready to come across, Connie? *(Stops short when he sees the* MAN *touching* CONNIE *and thinks the worst)*

CONNIE *(changing her mind):* Yes, I am, as a matter of fact. This man *(puts her arm around his neck)* is going to carry us over.

LINDY *(starting across):* Are you crazy? Do you think I'd let a man like that—?

CONNIE (MAN *has scooped her up and she delivers this line as he carries her):* A man like what?

LINDY *(his mouth drops open; then he laughs and shakes his head, realizing he is prejudiced also):* Come on, Susie. *(He carries her across, and they all exit making small talk.)*

LOVE ME, LOVE MY CHILD

Characters:
    Dovey McCoy Lee: *the mother-in-law*
    Iris Lee: *the daughter-in-law*

Setting:
    Each speaks as if explaining to a person who has asked about their relationship. They can be a distance apart or side by side, angled in opposite directions toward stationary focus points. Each seeks to justify her position but is aware at a deeper level that she should extend more grace to the other. Though they sometimes speak lines together, they are never aware of each other. They simply pause for thought while the other character speaks. Dovey is at a Bible study class. She holds a Bible. Even though she cannot read, it brings her comfort to have it in her lap.

Time:
    Before reunion

Props:
    2 chairs
    Bible

Dovey: Well . . .

Iris: Well . . .

Dovey: It's all her fault.

Iris: It's all her fault.

Dovey: She never

Iris: She never

Dovey: Acts like

Iris: Treats me like

Both: One of the family. Say we're having a meal together,

Dovey: She just stands and watches me. Never offers to help.

IRIS: She never tells me how I can help. If I start something, she just takes it away from me. What does it matter if the cucumbers are sliced or quartered? They taste the same either way. Looks like she'd notice how stupid she makes me feel.

DOVEY: She's eaten here dozens of times. Looks like she'd notice how I do things. But no.

IRIS: And no matter what new-fangled thing I buy to make things easier for her, she never uses any of them. And I ain't got money to waste.

DOVEY: And then there's them gifts she gives me. Well, I reckon she means well, but I just feel stupid using them 'cause I can't read the instructions to get the hang of how the things work.

IRIS: I pick what I think I'd want if I was her.

DOVEY: Not what I'd pick if I had my druthers. She'd know that if she took the trouble to find out what I like.

IRIS: If I ask her what she'd like she just says, "oh, anything, Iris."

DOVEY: If there's anything I should keep my mouth shut about, it's how to raise the kids. But I swear I can't hardly help it.

IRIS: And we always differ over the kids. The trouble is, well, she wants to tell me how she raised hers, and I just don't cotton to some of it.

DOVEY: The things them kids get by with! I'd straighten them out if I had a chance to keep them a month or two.

IRIS: I say, she's had her chance with her own brood. Now let me have mine. I'm young enough to remember how my mama did, and I got me some ideas about how to do it better.

DOVEY: I'm just trying to help her be a better mama. I can look back and see the mistakes I made, and I'd like to make it easier for her. And the young'uns too, God love 'em.

IRIS: After all, they're my kids.

DOVEY: After all, they're my grandkids. Does she think I'd steer her wrong?

IRIS: I'm just glad we don't live too close.

DOVEY: I tell you, I rue the day my boy moved 'em down to town. Don't the Good Book say, "Owe no man anything"? Hmmph! They think cash and carry is some kind of 'rithmetic problem. It's that city life—makes you want too much.

IRIS: There are things here in town I want for me and my family that they ain't got up on the mountain. Like the icehouse and the bakery and an actual church building. And especially the general store, 'cause I can go any day and buy what I forgot on grocery day. I'm a take-it-easy sort of person, and I don't want to bother my brain with keeping everything organized like she does.

DOVEY: "She." That's what she calls me, if you want to know something else. "She." "Her." "Your Mother."

IRIS: "She." *(Laughs slightly, embarrassed)* I never have knowed what to call her. I ask her once't soon after I married Jim, and she said to call her whatever I wanted to. Jim called her "Mother," so it didn't seem right for me to. I called my own mother "Mama," so that wouldn't do either. I noticed she always introduced me as just "Iris," so I thought maybe the best thing would be to just call her by her given name, Dovey.

DOVEY: "Dovey," she called me once't. Like just an acquaintance might. Was that all she wanted me to be?

IRIS: I was just Iris, the girl her son married, so she had to treat me tolerable.

DOVEY: Even though I had told her to call me what she liked—was that all the respect she had?

IRIS: She looked at me like I was a pagan. I knowed right then that she would never want me as her equal. We couldn't ever really be friends.

BOTH: It just about broke my heart.

DOVEY: Would this come between me and my boy?

IRIS: Would this come between me and my husband?

DOVEY: I had hoped . . .

IRIS: I had hoped . . .

BOTH: I could be . . .

DOVEY: Like a mother.

IRIS: Like a daughter.

BOTH: I had hoped she could be . . .

DOVEY: Like a daughter.

IRIS: Like a mother. But I can't get close to her. Like, I tried to explain to her once't that I really wanted to come to PawPaw's funeral, but I was just too sick.

DOVEY: But she ain't a daughter.

IRIS: Truth was, the doctor had put me to bed, afraid I'd miscarry. And I did, but we never told her. She was just too tore up over PawPaw.

DOVEY: Didn't even come to my old man's funeral.

IRIS: She didn't even come to our housewarming. To pay me back, I guess.

DOVEY: I try to be family and do things together, but I don't like to go down there when they're having some kind of party. Sometimes they play games where you have to read and write. And their friends come in all fancied up. I just feel like I embarrass her and Jim.

IRIS: It's embarrassing going on about private things like this. I shouldn't have started in on it.

DOVEY: Aw, I wouldn't have started in on all this if you hadn't asked us if there was anybody we didn't get along with.

IRIS: Just a minute, what are you saying to me? Who said that about my kid?

DOVEY: Yeah, I heard you read that verse. Here, turn my Bible to where you are and just let me hold it. Let's see, it was something like "He that hateth his brother is in darkness."*

IRIS: My Jamie? Why did they say they hated him?

DOVEY: But I don't *hate* her.

IRIS: I know he's not as smart as his sister. But that don't make no never mind.

DOVEY: I don't 'spect I could say I gen-u-winely love her.

IRIS: I love him just like he is.

DOVEY: She just provokes me to death.

IRIS: He ain't strange; he's just shy. Oh, people make me so mad I could die!

DOVEY: I don't know which one verse 14 is. Read it to me again. Oh, "Anyone who does not love remains in death."*

IRIS: Who said that? I'll scratch their eyes out! Love me, love my child.

DOVEY: "Everyone who loves the Father loves his child as well."* Well, I never thought about her like His child.

IRIS: Love God, love *His* child? Who, Jamie? Ohhh . . . Dovey. No, I can't say I love her just like she is.

DOVEY: Wait now; I've got that one memorized: "Behold what manner of love the Father hath bestowed upon us, that we should be called . . ."

IRIS: I reckon you're right. If I don't want nobody talking down about my child, God probably don't neither. 'Fact, I guess it really breaks His heart when I don't love one of the . . .

BOTH: children of God."*

(Both characters' focus points move higher for the last two lines, reflecting that this old saying has proven true in their own lives, as well as realizing that it can apply to God and His spiritual children as well.)

Iris: "When they're young they tromp on your apron strings, God;

Dovey: when they're grown they tromp on your heart."

*Scriptures paraphrased from 1 John 2:11; 3:1, 14; and 5:1 (KJV).

LORD HAVE MERCY

Characters:
Sam McCoy
Alice Golightly: *his sister*

Setting:
Sam has come to visit Alice in her home, which is a distance from him, farther up the mountain.

Time:
Before reunion

Pacing:
Midway through the sketch Alice cannot help but depart from friendly chat and begin to admonish Sam. They both understand that his behavior is a serious matter to her, but Sam can banter with her, which agitates her. Once this begins, pick up the pace and let it build. Otherwise it will lag and become boring. They are accustomed to snapping hasty retorts to one another, but Sam reaches his limit about three-quarters of the way through. There is an understood love between them that keeps them close despite their continuing mutual exasperation with one another.

SAM: Lordy, you never know what kids are thinking.

ALICE: You watch how you speak the Lord's name, Sam.

SAM: What? You always saying "Lord-a-mercy."

ALICE: Only in situations where He needs to have mercy.

SAM: Well, He did in this one, I guarantee. You think your young'uns is learning some sense, and then they just up and do something to prove you a liar. Benny—just on the way up here.

ALICE: What'd he do?

SAM: Him and Dan and little Ellen run on ahead. I stopped down at the spring a minute to get a drink of water.

(ALICE *looks at him with raised eyebrows.*)

SAM: Well, a drink. When I caught up to them—I can't believe this—they was off the path out in them waist-high weeds. I couldn't even see little Ellen, and just Dan's head. Benny was leading them around. They'd all fall down together, trying to flatten out a place, screaming and giggling.

ALICE: Lord-a-mercy, there's rattlers in there! Maybe copperheads too.

SAM: Shut your mouth. When I think about little ol' Ellen laying there and one of them snakes crawling over her curls, it's like an icicle down my shirt. I hollered, "Benny, you'ens get out of them weeds this minute! You know better."

ALICE: Did they skedaddle?

SAM: Nah. He hollered, "It's OK, Paw; don't worry." "It ain't OK. Get out of there. You gonna get bit." Then I seen Benny lift a big stick up over his head. "It's OK, Paw. I got the snake pole, just like you told me to always do. For protection. The snake pole's protecting us. I didn't forget."

ALICE *(laughs)*: What you been telling him, Sam?

SAM: Yeah, you laugh, Alice; but it wudn't funny. I went in there and snatched them up like fighting fire. Their skin went purty pale when I told them the pole was for protection 'cause you could hit snakes with it, not because it kept 'em away.

ALICE: Guess they stuck purty close to you after that.

SAM: Yep. Who would've dreamed they thought that? That a body could walk on purpose through a field of snakes, holding up a pole to protect him. Beats me. Benny reads too many fairy tales.

ALICE: I was just thinking . . .

SAM: What?

ALICE: Ain't that what you do, Sam?

SAM: Huh?

ALICE: Yeah, every time you come up here you gotta tell me how much moonshine you can hold, or brag about how you cheated somebody out of something. Or you done had you another woman—or worse. I'd call that walking around in the snakes' den.

SAM: Ahhh, a body's gotta have a little fun, Alice. Life is rough. I ain't no bad man. You know I was born again and sanctified in the blood several year ago.

ALICE: You think that protects you, don't you? You hold Jesus' cross up like a snake pole and think you can tramp anywhere you want to and still be safe. But they's poison in there waiting on you.

SAM: Well, they say that cross will give me everlasting life. That's right, ain't it? So even if I don't protect myself, you know, if I slip and take some chances now and then, I ain't gonna really die.

ALICE: There's such a thing as getting bit so bad and suffering so much you wish you was dead.

SAM: What you being so solemn about?

ALICE: 'Cause that cross didn't come easy and it didn't come cheap and you ought not to take it lightly, like it was a fairy tale. Snakes is real.

SAM: You think I'm gonna get bit?

ALICE: 'Lessen you straighten up.

SAM *(chuckles)*: If I did, would you be my nurse?

ALICE: No sirree.

SAM: Come on, now. You wouldn't want my blood on your hands, would you?

ALICE: It wouldn't be. You make your own choices.

SAM: Then why wouldn't you nurse a poor old ailing sinner? Afraid you'll get corrupted yourself?

ALICE: That ain't the reason.

SAM: Then why?

ALICE: 'Cause you would have had it coming. You been properly warned.

SAM: You mean I'd be getting what I deserved?

ALICE: Just precisely.

SAM: But they always told me grace covered everything.

ALICE: Then let Grace nurse you.

SAM: Now, Alice, I thought that's why Jesus died, so I don't get what I deserve.

ALICE: He shore didn't die so you can go out and do anything you happen to like!

SAM: Well, missy, are you so holy you're willing to get what you deserve?

ALICE: I never said that!

SAM: So you walk around in the snakes' den too.

ALICE: Sometimes.

SAM: So why should I get what I deserve and you not?

ALICE: You do it on purpose!

SAM: Don't you?

ALICE: Not as a way of life.

SAM: Well maybe I don't mean it to be my way of life either.

ALICE: Maybe.

SAM: I can remember having a hankering for meanness even when I was a little boy; you know, sort of ornery. Guess I was born that way.

ALICE: We all got a weakness of some kind. Don't mean you have to give in to it.

SAM: Maybe I try real hard, but it's just the way I am. Can't seem to help it.

ALICE: Hmph! Then you better watch out. And Lord have mercy on you.

SAM: You serious, Alice? If I got bit real bad, you wouldn't even . . .

ALICE: Wouldn't even what?

SAM: You know, come to my aid?

ALICE: I wouldn't touch you with a ten-foot pole.

SAM: Lord have mercy on you too.

TADGE

Character:
   Talmadge McCoy

Setting:
   Any

Time:
   After reunion

   My daughter just married a man that had two kids. They wasn't no talking her out of it. Of all the other things she might be, now she's a stepmother too. I wouldn't have wished it on her for nothing. I tried to tell her how it's gonna be:
   "You ain't my real mother, so you can't tell me what to do."
   "I bet my real maw would have been good to me."
   "One of these days I'll run away and go find her and we'll be real happy together."
   "My real mother was so pretty—smart too."
   "You just have to put up with us 'cause you wanted our daddy."
   "That ain't the way my maw would do it."
   Ah, they might be scared to say all of it out loud. But that don't mean they ain't thinking it. Matter of fact, being quiet is more dangerous than being sassy. To the mother 'cause she can't tell what's wrong and try to fix it. To the kid 'cause keeping all that bottled up like you was a jar makes it turn all moldy and cankered. A root of bitterness, the scripture calls it. It'll eat your innards out.
   I know how it is, 'cause I remember my mother. She was pretty and sweet and smart. Worked hard to give us a lot of life out of a little income. The way she made our garden grow, she was a regular Adam before the Fall. There was 13 of us kids, and she made all our clothes. The older kids got new ones, and the rest got hand-me-downs altered or darned or patched by hand. It was teejus [tedious] work. The bigger the older kids, the longer it took. I've laid there on my straw tick in the loft and watched her take them tiny stitches neat as a line of ants—half the night till the oil was gone out of the lamp. But she'd be acalling us as it was peeping daybreak with biscuits and gravy ready. Sometimes when I'd see her lay her sewing down with a big sigh and rest her head on her arms for a minute, or see her jab her finger 'cause of some old thick cloth, I thought my heart would bust right apart like the firewood I had to split. I done what little I could to help her, but I dreamed of being rich someday and giving her things to make life easier. Paw said, "Tadge, you're too soft-hearted.

He said it was a woman's job to see to running the home. And then my maw died. I missed her so bad that it was almost like she was still there. Until my stepmother moved in.

She never had a chance. And she didn't even know why; didn't know that it weren't even exactly her fault. They hadn't been married but a month or so when one night I looked down over the loft and do you know what I saw setting on the table—right where I used to see my maw rest her poor head, with the little strands of hair worked out of her bun and sticking to her neck? A sewing machine. You might as well have hit me across the face with a razor strop, because my teeth began to clench and my jaw tightened all the way down to the pit of my stomach. She became the enemy, 'cause Paw bought her what he would never buy my mother. Wellsir, because I became surly, directly she got to be surly back to me. I begrudged her everything, so she was stingy with me. And since I couldn't stand her, she didn't like me neither.

Sometimes I wonder if she could have seen her way clear to like me whether I liked her or not, to be kind to me even when I said hateful things, if she could have give me the biggest piece of cake or not tattled on me sometimes, I wonder if it would have made a difference in how I felt. If she could have understood that I was acting rotten because I was feeling rotten, and not because I was rotten. If she could have knowed that I didn't have nowhere to shoot my anger and she was an easier target than Paw, I would have soon run out of bullets, most likely. I think if she could have loved me in spite of the things I did, I could have learned to tell her why I did them and give her a chance to explain herself. But silence was like snow covering a big mudhole, and they wasn't no getting up that road at all.

I still find it hard to like her, even if she has been dead for years. But I guess I do sympathize with her a little more now that I'm older. I can see she took care of us purty well. I reckon it warn't easy to take us on her family.

Which brings me back to my daughter's new family. So I'm gonna tell her that she for certain shore married some heartaches, and took on more obligations than the ones she can see. She made that choice fair and square, so she's just gotta remember that she followed her heart and the heart was made to love. Even if it aches, even if it breaks, a heart's gotta love. That's what makes it strong—strong enough to take all the spiteful blades and bullets and cheap shots and still stand there firm like a fort. That way, iffen a body sees he can't get around it or through it, he's just liable to ask to come in through the gate. 'Specially if he's starving.

Yep, stepfamilies is gonna have more fights than normal. But shoot, forewarned is forearmed. She's just gotta remember that love, with no strings attached, is the surest way to win a fight. Mind you, I didn't say the easiest way. But since I love her, although I might not agree with her choice, I've decided to be around and try to make it easier for her if I can. You know, help hold the fort when she needs me. I just gotta remember, like the Good Book says, love never fails.

GEORGE

Character:
GEORGE McCOY (Uncle Jed is imaginary)

Setting:
Stage represents the top of a mountain. GEORGE is sitting on a large boulder. The stage floor represents its flat top, and the rest of the rock is imaginary.

Time:
Before reunion

Props:
Rifle (optional)

(Startled) Oh! Why, howdy, Uncle Jed. I didn't expect to see you up here. You caught me off guard. Bet you been on over the other side ciphering out a stand of timber for somebody. Yeah, I allowed as much. Me? Oh, I been squirrel hunting. Seems like it's a little better in these woods up here at the top, but I ain't done no good yet. Set yourself down here a minute and rest and tell me how you be. Oh, I been tolerable.

Rock's good and warm, ain't it? Yep, Auger Rock's about the purtiest place hereabouts. You can see a whole lot more daylight up here. See where a body's been and where he might could go if he had a mind to. I was aiming to have my dinner here. I brung me some fatback 'tween two pieces of cornbread. I laid it right there, but then I decided to move my rifle-gun over yonder, and bless Chucky Jack if the end of it didn't knock my dinner plumb off. Might nigh fell off trying to catch it. Yep, it was a mite scary, but that ain't why you startled me. Nope, I was deep in thought about something. I was over to that meeting in John Holler yesterday where all them folk been getting revived up. Preacher's talking about a verse that said "Deliver them that are drawn unto death" (Proverbs 24:11). Said it was like Old Aaron that took a stand between the living and the dead, delivering them back from destruction of the plague. Or like Moses stood between the people and God's wrath so He wouldn't destroy them. Well it come to me, if that had been somebody falling off, would I have reached to get them as quick as I did my fatback? You now, if a body tripped on a root or something on the path and come tumbling down, would I stand here between him and death and risk my life to stop him? Why, he could fall plumb down to my house, scare the sass out of Sarah Mae.

(Pause)

I seen sis do it before: stand between life and death. Tend the ones with typhoid or something and make the family get out to stay safe. 'Course the preacher was talking about holding them back from falling clear to eternal destruction, but I don't think I've done much of that neither. So I said to myself, "George, it's a shame you and Sarah Mae both had to go off like the prodigal son and break your maw's heart. And you know she stood between you and doom with her prayers and the way she lived. It's been way a long time ago since you come to your senses. So when you gonna remember what it's like to hoe the row that some of them other prodigals are in? When you gonna care about the danger they're in unawares? When you gonna get in there and let them laugh at you and cuss you, maybe try to kill you, so you can stand between life and them walking on off the real Rock, blessed be His name?"

You know, Uncle Jed, if I'm really grateful that somebody done it for me, I'm obliged to do it for somebody else. And I got one or two in mind right now. *(Pause)* Sarah Mae writ a poem about us prodigals. She ever tell it to you? I shore will. Goes like this:

>Because he loved the prodigal,
>The father cried that day;
>>Yet paid him half
>>Because he asked
>And watched him walk away.
>I've been to that far country, Lord,
>Why, I'm that same young man:
>>Won't be denied,
>>And showed my pride
>In using my own plan.
>How many times have You watched me Lord,
>Leave the secure household?
>>Known the results
>>Felt the insults,
>But choosing not to scold?
>I'm that man when he wasted, Lord;
>I have been hungry too;
>>I've fed the swine
>>And toed the line
>For lesser lords than You.
>Yes, I'm that man in deepest shame;
>Oh, how I've felt his pain!
>>But, Lord, praise You
>>I'm that man too
>When he came home again!

By the way, you on your way home, Uncle Jed? I mean your real home on them golden streets? Well, that's good to know. Me too. But right now I'm going to my old English Mountain home and get me a bite to eat. See if I can get something between me and this growling stomach. Maybe Sarah Mae'll have some poke sallet cooked up.

(As he exits) Maybe I'll see you over to the meeting. Yeah, and maybe I'll have somebody with me too.

DOVEY

Character:
   Dovey McCoy Lee

Setting:
   Any

Time:
   Anytime between 1918 and 1950

Props:
   Bag of stick candy *(suck one stick occasionally as stage business)*

   Did anybody ever tell you just how stingy you are? Well they did me. And I was the one that done the telling and the listening. I told myself. Out loud. 'Cause up till then I hadn't knowed and I wanted to be shore and remember what it felt like. I said, "Dovey, don't never forget this."
   It was Christmastime and every year there would be a party for us kids down at the schoolhouse. We would chop down a cedar tree somewheres in the woods close by. For days we woulda been making big long strings of popcorn to decorate it up. We'd pick little bunches of red berries and tie on, and little cloth bows if our maws had any scraps left over from quilting. That tree all gussied up was a wonder to look at.
   All the mamas and daddies would throw in together and try to make Christmas a little out of the ordinary. Maw always said God coming to live with the likes of us was shore nuff out of the ordinary, and we ought to celebrate it proper-like. I 'member one time somebody that had left the mountain and worked in a bakery in town sent us up some loaves of white yeast bread for the party. That is one time I woulda liked for Jesus to be there and fix it so's we had 12 basketsful left over. It was so light and sweet compared to our biscuits and fried bread, we all thought it was cake. And did we make pigs of ourselves! Sooey! Sooey!
   The parents always wrapped up a little present for their own kids and put it under the tree at the party. One year we got an orange and a banana. We didn't always get bananas. Usually we got one orange and maybe two more on Christmas morning. Sometimes with a stick of sassafras candy. So I was tickled with my banana. That is, till I saw what Dorcas Foy got—a paper poke full of candy! Her paw had bartered something with Mr. Spencer, the man that owned the rolling store, and got his girl some candy and some fruit besides. Why, the

closest I usually got to candy was when we made molasses and I could stick a piece of cane in the pot to lick.

The bad thing was, she eat a piece right in front of us, and let us all look in her sack real close, so the smell just made you want it that much more. I can tell you for a fact, don't linger long over something you know you can't have. It will git you in all manner of trouble and make you miserable. I gar-un-tee the "want to" will keep coming back, but don't let it dally for one second. You can't keep it from knocking on the door of your mind, but you got the say on what comes in. Slam the door!

Me and Dorcas was always purty good friends, so I'd keep sidling up to her during the games and allowing as how I shore did have a hankering for some of that candy. Not a whole piece or nothing—maybe just a bite. Then I tried saying I'd do most anything for a bite. Directly I moved on into how selfish a body would have to be to own a whole sackfull of candy and not share any. And finally I said that selfish body was her and stomped off. I thought I had seen the height of selfishness until we was sitting around sucking our oranges and I looked across the room and seen Dorcas had something stuck in the top of her'n. She was sucking her orange through a peppermint stick! If that didn't just put the tassel on the corn! Oh, I could have lit in on her and walloped her good. And in my mind I fumed at her, at the whole unfair world—which for me right then was made up of that little room. I stopped being Dorcas's friend. I got real holy then—to hide my pain, I guess—and thanked God I wuhdn't that all-fired stingy.

I was wrong. The day come, as them kind of days will, when you least expect it. I guess the crops had done mighty good that year or something. Anyway, Paw didn't let us go when it was the week for Spencer's Rolling Store to come. We was real disappointed. It was sorta like a party. See, we never knowed exactly when the store could get there, so in the winter they built up a big bonfire and all the neighbors would sing and catch up on everybody's news while they waited. Maybe you could spark a little with your beau too. But we was made to stay home that time. Come Christmas morning, we each had two oranges, two bananas, and a little paper poke of candy! Peppermint sticks, licorice, coconut drops, chocolate mountains, orange slices—what treasures! I aimed to make mine last a long time.

Later Christmas Day, Pee Wee Barrett come over to play. I was the only kid inside, and Maw told me to give him a piece of my candy. She might as well have asked for the moon. I said, "What candy, Maw?" She took me out on the back porch and told me I should be ashamed of myself—how Pee Wee didn't have no family and just moved around from pillar to post—how kindly it would be to share a little something with him for Christmas.

"You share your'n with him," I said.

"Well, yens got all the candy, but I did give him one of my oranges."

"Well, that's all he needs then. A body that ain't got nothing should appreciate that," I said.

I didn't want to give up my treasure. She didn't force me, but she did try to sway me by telling me that Paw had give it to me out of the goodness of his heart. Maybe I'd give him half a stick, then? No.

She didn't say no more, but she turned and looked at me as she went in the door. I seen a tear come down her cheek, and it was shining like a jewel. Put me in mind of something shiny and glittery I'd seen before, but I couldn't think where. What was it? Seemed like it was right at the tip of my noggin. And then the memory just washed over me all at once't. Kindly like a fainting spell does. It was that sparkle in Dorcas's eyes that year she got all the candy. That awful gleam as she looked at her treasure and wouldn't even look at me. I can feel to this day how bad I wanted her candy, and how bad it hurt not to get it. I felt sick at my stomach—like I never wanted no more candy—and a few jewels of my own was coming out my eyes and down my cheeks.

I saw Pee Wee way down the path, and I lit out running fast as I could, hollering for him to wait. Just as I got to him I stumbled and fell. Spilt my candy everywhere. Pee Wee helped me pick all the pieces up and never so much as put one tiny one in his mouth. I give him the only clean, whole stick left and said, "Merry Christmas, Pee Wee." And when he said Merry Christmas back at me, I seen something shining in his eyes.

That—that was the day I told myself just how stingy I was. That other year before, when I thought I wuhdn't, I made a big mistake. I thought that the more you had, the easier it would be to share it. But it ain't so. If you're stingy with one thing, you'll be stingy with a lot. Which, if I had bothered to pay it some heed, is what the Bible said all along.

DOOR TO HEAVEN

Characters:
　　Sarah Mae McCoy
　　Bart McCoy

Setting:
　　Front porch of Sarah Mae's mountain home

Time:
　　Early in 1930

Props:
　　Medicinal powder tied in a rag

Bart *(enters in a winded state, calling)*: Sarah Mae, Sarah Mae!

Sarah Mae *(enters porch from interior; slaps her thighs and whoops in her characteristic fashion)*: Howdy, Bart. How you feeling?

Bart: Poorly; mighty poorly.

Sarah Mae: Root medicine didn't help none?

Bart: Well, it eases me some. So I thought I'd come and trouble you for some more.

Sarah Mae: Sakes alive! You done used all I give you?

Bart: I told you, it's bad. I'm tuckered out just walking up from my place.

Sarah Mae: Well set yourself down then. You didn't have to strain yourself—I would have been by there tomorrow.

Bart: Couldn't wait.

Sarah Mae: Should have sent one of the young'uns then.

Bart: Aw, Sarah Mae, no use in them fretting over me. I don't really want them to know.

Sarah Mae: They know you're sick, Bart.

Bart: You know that ain't what I mean.

SARAH MAE: No, I don't.

BART: Yes you do.

SARAH MAE: No I don't neither.

BART: You know what I'm talking about. I don't want them to know I'm . . .

SARAH MAE: You're what?

BART: That I'm . . . uh . . .

SARAH MAE: What?

BART: You know.

SARAH MAE: I do not. And that just proves it ain't so. You can't even say the word.

BART: I can so.

SARAH MAE: Cannot.

BART: Can too.

SARAH MAE: Won't, then.

BART: Will so.

SARAH MAE: Won't. Ain't so anyway.

BART: Is so.

SARAH MAE: No it ain't.

BART: Is!

SARAH MAE: Ain't!

BART: Hush up! You're aggravating me to death!

SARAH MAE: Don't you blame it on me!

(Silence)

BART: I'm dying, Sarah Mae.

SARAH MAE: I know. *(Sad pause)* 'Sides, don't you think it's better to tell them so they can get prepared?

BART: How they gonna do that?

SARAH MAE: I don't know. I just always thought it was a double jolt if somebody's death comes unexpected—without warning you. I kindly like my thunder and my lightning to be a little distance apart.

BART: Well, a body don't always get what they want. I'm proof of that.

SARAH MAE: Some say kids understand better than grown-ups.

BART: I say kids should stay kids just as long as they can.

SARAH MAE: But you could tell them good-bye. Tell them what you want them to do.

BART: I want them to be happy. That's why I ain't telling them. And that's up to me to decide and nobody else.

SARAH MAE: Yep, a body's gotta do what they think is best. But they don't have to expect everybody to agree with them.

BART: It's my decision.

SARAH MAE: It shore is.

BART: It's my kids!

SARAH MAE: That's right!

BART: It's my life! *(Long pause)* It's hard enough to think about living. I don't think I could take them moping around, worrying and "getting prepared" as you call it. 'Sides, seems like I'm the one needs to be prepared.

SARAH MAE: I reckon so.

BART: What do you think heaven's like, Sarah Mae?

SARAH MAE: Oh, I reckon it's a wonder, Bart.

BART: Yeah, but lately I been trying to get a better picture of it in my mind. Do you think it's just like this, only greener and shinier with no weeds, with beautiful flowers and big, juicy fruit? You think there'll be dogs to pet and horses to ride? Or do you suppose it's a different kind of place entirely where you sit on clouds and wear robes and play harps?

SARAH MAE: I don't know them things. But I reckon it don't matter.

BART: It's just a little scary, not knowing what it will be like.

SARAH MAE: Well, Bart, for you I think heaven will be a whole lot like a auty-mo-bile.

BART: A auty-mobile? You got some mighty strange ideas.

SARAH MAE: No sir, they was your ideas. Remember when somebody first told you what a car looked like?

BART: Yeah, it was Old Man Rhinehart—seen them over in Asheville.

SARAH MAE: He told you they had doors.

BART: Doors! *(They have a good laugh at the memory.)* And the only kind of door I could see it having in my mind was like a door to a house.

SARAH MAE: That was all you could talk about for weeks. Worried us to death wondering how something that tall could roll around on four wheels.

BART: It puzzled me, all right. I thought you went up some steps and then walked through a regular seven-foot door.

SARAH MAE: Sort of like a house on wheels?

BART: I couldn't imagine, really.

SARAH MAE: Yes, you could imagine; that's what worried you.

BART: Well, when they told me you got in it through doors, naturally I thought of the kind of doors I'm used to.

SARAH MAE: Yep.

BART: When I finally saw one, wasn't nothing like I thought. I was plumb amazed.

SARAH MAE: Well, I'm glad you remember that, Bart, 'cause that's what I think about heaven. You're trying to imagine it by the things you're used to, and I don't think there's any comparison. I think you're gonna be amazed, pure-T amazed and in wonderment. *(Whoops and slaps her thighs)* Heaven and auty-mobiles—they both transport you! So don't be worrying your mind. You probably too stubborn to die, anyway, so don't be worrying me with your talk, either.

BART: Give me some more of your medicine, and I won't.

(SARAH MAE *goes inside.* BART *quotes Bible verses, etc.* SARAH MAE *returns and hands him the powder tied in a rag.)*

BART: Bye, Sarah Mae.

SARAH MAE: Bye, Bart.

BART *(walks away; just before he exits):* Ain't you gonna see me to the door? *(Exits laughing)*

SARAH MAE *(smiles and shakes her head slightly in recognition of his spunk; to herself):* Yeah, Bart, I'm afraid I will.

CITIES, KINGS, WEEPING, AND THINGS

Character:
　　Sarah Mae McCoy

Setting:
　　Her home in the mountains; she can be inside, on the porch, or in the yard, but give her some chore or business to do as she speaks.

Time:
　　Before reunion

　　I don't have no desire to ever leave these mountains. Way back in here, people call it the wilderness, say there's a lot of wild things that live back here, and they're right. But I shore feel safer than I do down in the city. Yeah, been to some, visiting my kin from the East, and I'm here to tell you they got some really wild things in town.

　　They took me in one of them moving picture houses. Well, there was a woman up there in front of everybody dressed like I ain't never seen, and she caused these two men to get up and fight like wildcats. I thought they was going to kill each other, and not a man in that place was brave enough to get up there and break them up. I kept yelling for somebody to do something and everybody kept telling me to sit down and hush up. My brother took me out in the little parlor at the front and told me to calm down 'cause it weren't real. "Don't tell me; I saw it with my own eyes!" He said, "Sarah Mae, we told you these are pictures." Well, they did look a little fuzzy, but I hadn't ever seen any pictures that big. Besides, the people in them was moving around. He said that's why they was called moving pictures; didn't I remember him explaining it to me? I guess so, but I couldn't get used to it. I couldn't help it—I would tell them out in the seats to quit laughing at the people up there right to their faces, and then they would all laugh at me.

　　And another thing in the city, even the people rush around like wild things. Have to be on their job at a certain minute and quit at a certain minute. Shoot, they even had a little war down there at my brother's city 'cause a group called the union went wild trying to keep people from working. Had the National Guard and police out. Some people got maimed or killed. Does that sound civilized to you?

And they ain't no night down there. Soon as it gets dusky dark, big lights come on up on poles along the street. They say it makes it harder on the wild human things that sneak around in the city and get into meanness. Then the houses have electric lights and the stores, and there's lights on the auty-mobiles. There just ain't no dark.

A train runs right through the middle of town, and people push and shove each other trying to get on it. There's a mill of some kind that lets off a stink you can smell all over town. Just shows me why old Abraham didn't get riled up when Lot chose the city to live in and left him out in the country. Abraham knowed it—cities is dangerous. I was glad to get back to the mountains. Don't care if I ever go back.

One thing about going, though, I never knowed how many purty mountains there are till I got to ride off in an auty-mobile and look back at them. Ooooweee! Blue, purple, green, gray ridges as far as you can see right to the edge of the earth. Why, Old English wouldn't be big as half a flea in all that. I thought of David when I saw that, how amazed he was in the Psalms that God could look out over all them heavens and still know who he was.

David was up in the mountains a good bit hisself. Yep, I was sitting up at the water trough pondering the other day about how many things in the Bible happened on mountains: The Ten Commandments, the first sight of the Promised Land, Elijah's fire, Jesus' temptation, the Sermon on the Mount, the Transfiguration, the Ascension. Lots of times Jesus just went up in the mountains to pray.

Had you ever thought about Jesus being the Son of David and how they was both kings who went up the same mountain when their people put them out? Yep, I was reading a verse there in the Second Book of Samuel one day, and it was right after Easter. I thought to myself, "This seems awfully familiar; I believe we read this in the Easter services." So I looked up that scripture and what do you know—they could have been twins. That's right. King David's son Absalom took and started a rebellion against him, so David had to leave Jerusalem. I done told you about cities, didn't I? David said, "Let the Lord do what seems good to Him." Then he crossed the Kidron Brook and went up the Mount of Olives weeping as he went. Well now, the Son of David, Jesus, came to His own people as the King they had been waiting for, but they didn't accept Him. They was making plans to kill Him in Jerusalem. You know what the Bible says He done? He crossed the Kidron Brook and went up the Mount of Olives; He told God to do whatever He willed, and He wept. But Jesus was the shore-nuff forever King. See, David was a man after God's own heart, but Jesus was a man who *was* God's own heart. Nobody rejects Him and gets by with it, even to this day.

So I got to thinking about how many times I had rejected Him or hurt His heart. How some of my friends just pure-T reject Him still, and I ain't gone to no trouble to talk them into believing, or even wept over them. So I don't guess you have to live in the city to be in danger or meanness. I still say it's more likely, just because you have more chances there to get into it.

You know how things can just get to you sometimes and seem so real it's scary? Well that day it was just like God had hisself some of them moving pictures. I could see poor old King David crossing my creek and trudging up my mountain, crying, leaving his kingdom behind. As soon as he clumb out of sight, there was Jesus following him: across my creek, up my mountain, crying His heart out like a king shouldn't ever have to do. 'Specially 'cause of the likes of me. I commenced to cry then to think that kings and even God had to suffer sometimes and give up things and be brought low for the sake of other people. So it seemed the only fitting thing for me to do was cross my creek and climb my mountain, tears streaming down my face, and pray for all us folk that think we want to be kings instead of servants.

Scripture references: Genesis 13:8-12; 2 Samuel 15:23-30; Matthew 26:36-40; John 18:1

MYSTERIOUS YEAR

Character:
    Tadge McCoy

Setting:
    Any

Time:
    Before reunion

It was the year Sarah Mae finally give up the ghosts. I don't mean hers; she's 'bout as alive as you can get. Ghostses I should say. Of Charlie, her first love; Janie, her dead sister; and our dear departed mama. She had some kind of visitation of the Spirit up at the water trough that caused her to quit mooning over one and grieving over t'other. It was a mysterious year. The year I first come to believe in miracles.

See, I had been too smart for that foolishment. Common sense is what counts. Everwhat you plant is what comes up; prune a tree at the wrong time, and it won't blossom; dig taters at the wrong time, and they'll rot; get one of the bad sicknesses, and you die. Maw died. Paw died; his new wife Birdie too. They said Old Spotted Trudy, my pet sheep, was dying. That's just how things are. Do this, do that, you get this here. It's just like 'rithmetic—simple, no arguing with it.

I did know something was different about Sarah Mae—a whole lot of something. Since she's the oldest, she had sort of been our mama for a while. And she didn't take to that any more than we did. But that year she commenced to be more and more like Maw, and the change was just more than I could believe, hardly. She'd say, "Tadge, let me explain it to you," but it always had a big dollop of God in it, and that's when I quit listening. All them miracles in the Bible, why I had done growed up too much to believe in them.

That year, 1910 it was, it snowed on Easter and folk begin to say that it was going to be a strange year. Shore enough, these spooky little lights begin to appear hereabouts. Just kind of floating over the holler, and then jumping almost to the top of the mountains, jerky-like. Sometimes they would look like they was only a whoop and a holler from you, but if you chased them they might jump treetop-high and seem far away. Every time they showed up, all the creeks flooded within a week. I mean floods like never was seen here.

Then there was the mystery of Farrell Coley. I had been playing with him since I was three or four. He was born blind, but you couldn't hardly tell it unless you just knowed it. He was almost a regular feller—didn't talk like he was blind or nothing. Anyway, there come this man over to the church what said he was a faith healer. Farrell's mama took him over there, and they prayed over him about three nights. The healer told him to go to the mineral springs and wash his face. Well, the next time I saw Farrell, he saw me. Nobody ever knowed if it was the healer or the springs that done it. It just stayed a mystery.

And then there was the mystery of the moonshine. Or more like the mystery of me—all growed up now, like I said. Well, there was them friends what allowed that if I was so all-fired big it was time I come one night and sample their mountain dew. I had done made up my mind several years back that I would stay away from that stuff. Paw and Birdie had told me how it could put a craving on you that you could never get rid of. But mostly I had seen firsthand what nobody coulda told me. And that was how one of my uncles would lower hisself 'cause of liquor. I don't know which was worse: what he would do to get it, or what he done after he got it. I didn't want no part of either one. Like I said, I believed in common sense, and that was most precisely not it.

But what does a 17-year-old boy do when his pals keep on at him, calling him names, the best of which was coward? Paw said it was simple: just tell 'em, "No." Well I did for about six months, all the time having nightmares about being laughed at. Then one of them told me that Mary Faye just so admired boys that didn't pay so much attention to old silly rules and was more interested in having a good time. She specially liked the way Bobby sparked with her after he had a few drinks. And he was so brave taking the risk of getting caught at his age. Well I was sorta sweet on Mary Faye, and it didn't take long before I agreed to go with them.

I told Sarah Mae I was going to revival meeting over the next holler, and I meant to. I put on my best clothes and went along with the fellers in an old horsecart. We went farther than I planned, but I still figured I could have one or two drinks and still get to the meeting. But two of the drinks is really all I remember, 'cept in a blur. Bunch of laughing, hollering, singing. The next thing I recollect is being sick on my stomach—bad sick—and fretting about throwing up on my good shirt; then fretting because I couldn't quit throwing up. That's the last I remember till I woke up by myself in the middle of the night—way long about three o'clock, I reckon. The fire had gone out; I was freezing and feeling mighty poorly.

I found my coat and started walking. That got me sorta woke up enough to notice that I could see a path. I knowed it weren't time for the full moon, but the state I was in, I could have seen anything. Shore enough, when I come out of the trees into a little clearing, I saw the biggest star I had ever laid eyes on. Four, maybe five times as big. And to beat all, it had a big long tail that went plumb across the sky, blazing like it was on fire. Shocked me so I couldn't even scream—scared the breath out of me. It was almost enough to sober me up. But not quite, I reckon, 'cause I begin to laugh then. "Looky here! It's the Star of Bethlehem!" I hollered, and just went into a fit of laughter again. "Here comes the wise man!" I laid down my coat and picked up a rock and strutted across that field like I was a king. "I'm following the star!" And I changed direction to face the head of the star.

Sarah Mae found me the next morning asleep just a few feet from the back steps. She rolled her eyes up at the smell, but she didn't say nothing much. Like I said, she was different now. She did make me wash my own clothes.

Later that day everybody was acting strange, kindly like they had a lid on them. But I found out it wuhdn't because of me. My big star had been real; everybody had seen it, and the agreement was that it meant the end of the world. That sorta helped to put some muscle behind a promise I made earlier that morning, to never touch another drop. And one miracle is, I've kept that promise, 'cause I really did love the taste of it. And because of that night, I learned how brave and sensible it can be to say that little miracle word, "No."

The star come back for several nights. 'Course, it warn't the end of the world. Next time the rolling store come around and we got our *Kansas City Star*—heh, heh, how do you like that, *Star?*—we found out it was called Halley's Comet and that it wouldn't come back for 75 year. I don't reckon I'll be alive then, so I shore am proud I seen it. For more reasons than one. I don't doubt the Bible no more. Since I seen Halley's Comet, I'm a pure-T believer that the wise men had a miracle star to guide them.

And the biggest miracle was that I made it home at all. Me and my brothers went to hunt my coat a couple days later. We found it in a field, where I laid it when I switched directions to pretend I was following the star. If I had kept going straight, likely I would have walked right off a great high place they call Skull and Bones, just a few yards ahead.

But that first morning, I still had a question for my sister. "By the way, Sarah Mae, what made you first see the comet anyway, in the middle of the night like that?"

"Oh," she said, "I forgot to tell you, Tadge. Old Spotted Trudy didn't die after all. And she birthed her new little lamb last night."

Like I said, it was a mysterious year.

ALICE

Character:
   Alice McCoy Golightly

Setting:
   Her yard or porch

Time:
   Before reunion

Props:
   Shoes to polish
   OR
   A stick to hold

   The first little nip that come in the air, Paw got all us young'uns together in a line, as usual. It was time to buy our new pair of shoes for the next year. 'Less, of course, we could wear the next biggest kid's old one, which wuhdn't hardly ever the case. Either they was wore through or the wrong size. Not that the new ones fit perfect either. See, we didn't go down to town with him and try them on. We had chores and school and such, and he had business and couldn't be fooling with us.
   So he laid a good sturdy stick down beside every foot and measured it off, plus what he figured was enough growing room, and that's where he cut the stick. Then he went off to buy shoes that fit, more or less, each of his sticks.
   Usually he was extra careful with the sticks, but one year the wagon lost a wheel and he had some trouble, nearly sliding off the bench when it tilted that-away, and even more trouble getting it fixed. Anyway, he thought he had broke one of the sticks, but he wuhdn't certain. He told the man at the general store that if it had got broke, it was shore a clean break. Before he would buy a pair to fit that stick, he made the man promise he could swap them if they didn't fit.
   We was all buzzing around him like june bugs on a string, grabbing our new shoes. I couldn't tell mine felt no different from the old ones. But they matched the stick with my initials. 'Course I didn't say nothing to Paw. My paw warn't the kind you say much to, and shorely not to question his judgment. And more's the pity, he didn't say nothing neither, 'cause he was just precisely not the kind of man to let on he might make a mistake.
   So I went around wearing the wrong shoes 'cause I felt like I had to almost, and I only got more miserable as the year went on. You know the feeling,

don't you? Just a mite uncomfortable at first. So you think, "Aw, I can stand it." You hate to complain, you know. You should be grateful and all like that. But the longer you wear that shoe that don't fit, the worse it hurts. You've had that feeling, ain't you? Something just pushing you in from all sides, squeezing tighter and tighter, cramping you up. Don't have no give a'tall. No room to move, just shaping your foot however it wants to. And you get fidgety and cranky and start to wonder if you can even walk any more, or if you even want to. But you're ashamed to let anybody see your tears.

And there's people, you know, that you look up to, or that you're scared of, and they say you need to wear shoes. So you wear 'em and you walk in 'em even though it don't hardly feel like a normal walk. And you're knowing all the time that these shoes don't fit you, but if you don't wear them, who will? Everybody else has their own shoes. Best of all, or maybe worst of all, you keep on grinning like the pain wuhdn't even there.

The sad thing was, I found out later that my sister's shoes was too big. Her feet didn't grow none that year, and she stuffed a rag in the toe every day. But she didn't say nothing neither. If we had told each other how we was hurting, we could have swapped shoes and walked along real easy, not to mention happy.

But the saddest thing of all was, whether I could swap with my sister or not, I didn't have to walk around like that. It was just me that thought I had to. I could have had a pair of shoes that fit me. My daddy had already made the arrangements. All I had to do was ask him.

FAMILY REUNION

Production Notes

This McCoy family reunion takes place in 1930 in the hard-packed dirt sideyard of the homeplace, where Sarah Mae and her brother George still live. The piece can stand on its own, but those who have seen the other sketches in the book will recognize characters and references to events (such as Lawrence's resurrection one year before) that should enhance their experience.

With so many people onstage, this play should be a challenge for the director. Happily, however, reunions are always a confusion of movement and noise. Just make sure the characters are visible as they speak and that others direct their focus to the speakers. To make it more realistic, the script intentionally includes a couple of conversations that take place simultaneously. When not directly involved, characters may engage in preparations in the background or sit and listen while whittling, breaking beans, peeling fruit, doing needlework, and so forth. More of the children can return near the end if you desire.

This play is an excellent opportunity for mutual appreciation and understanding between generations, not only those who will interact as its cast (ages 4 through 89), but those of another time as well. It depicts part of the delightful culture and flavor of life in a certain section of eastern Tennessee. If you have access to antique implements, spinning wheels, cider mills, and so forth, or antique toys, make use of them in the action to add to the mood and the learning experience. Perhaps the most interesting and fun is the chance to introduce another generation to some older songs. Some are suggested; you may substitute or add as many others as you wish. The older folks will almost certainly enjoy the nostalgia. If you can cast people who play appropriate instruments, by all means add them.

The total effect will be enhanced if the play can be staged so that the audience feels that they are a part of the reunion. Consider staging it in-the-round, or have some minor characters seated out with the audience while peeling fruit. They could even give slices to audience members. Some entrances and exits might be made down the aisles. Uncle Bruce could come out and find a Mason jar of moonshine under a seat in the front row. Definitely indicate that the audience sing along on some of the songs. In the final scene, the cast could sing another chorus of "Will the Circle Be Unbroken?" while their circle breaks in the middle and opens. The actor on each end would then reach his free hand toward the audience in invitation.

Four entrances are suggested: UR—From the house. DL—From the path. Those arriving from out of town or from lower elevations use this main entrance. DR—To the front yard. UL—To the orchard and path to the spring and cave. Either of these could also be DR beyond the yard.

FAMILY REUNION

Characters:
Sarah Mae
George
Lawrence and Florence, Joe, Bo, Zoe
Dovey and Jim, Iris, Jessie
Sam, Benny, Dan, Ellen
Alice and Dexter, Priestly
Carmel
Talmadge and Eve, Silas, Shirley, Franklin, June
Lindy, John Ed, Zelbert, Daisy Nell
Uncle Bruce
Prudence and Dakota, Wyoming, Virginia, Nebraska
Othey and Eulabelle, Grover, Delbert, Billy Roy, Bessie Jean

The following family members are not mentioned, but can appear as nonspeaking:

Zack
Elizabeth
Mary Lou
Uncle Jed

Time:
1930

Props:
Felled tree trunks, large rocks, tin tubs, barrels, and so forth; long boards for makeshift tables
Various items for stage business: bowls, pans, knives, vegetables and fruit, needlework, whittling objects
Broom (mountain variety)
Straight chairs
Stick of medium size, able to be broken over the knee
Huckleberry box or whip made from tree bark
Clover or daisies for a chain
Large handkerchief
Two large food baskets
Pocketknife
Suggested items to dress the stage, or for stage business:
    Antique farm implements
    Churns

Cider mill
Quilting frame
Mason jars
Bushel and half-bushel baskets
Tow sacks and feed sacks
Musical instruments: fiddles, Autoharps, zithers, harmonicas, Jew's harps, spoons, jug to blow on, guitars

(GEORGE *is setting up large sections of felled tree trunks or piles of large rocks, or tin tubs, barrels, etc., to serve as the base for picnic tables. Long boards will be placed side by side on these to serve as the tabletops. He sings "Farther Along." Near the end,* LAWRENCE *enters from the path and joins in on the last line or two.*)

GEORGE: Howdy, Lawrence. You understand it all, don't you? You already been farther along. What's it like?

LAWRENCE: You know I don't talk about that, George.

GEORGE: But I'm your brother.

LAWRENCE: Not to nobody. But I will give you a howdy. How you been?

GEORGE: Fair-to-middlin', I reckon. If you ain't gonna answer my questions, just get over here and help me get these tables up.

LAWRENCE *(he does so):* How many's coming?

GEORGE: Don't know yet. Some already here. Sure to be a passel of 'em. Family just keeps on growing. Where's your folk?

LAWRENCE: They'll be along directly. You know, we could have the reunion somewhere that's easier to get to. That mountain gets steeper every year.

GEORGE: Well now, Sarah Mae's our oldest sister, and I'm next, so yens can just come here. 'Sides, everybody wants to come back where Maw and Paw lived, God rest their souls.

LAWRENCE: Yeah, it's good to be home. Ain't changed much 'cept for the new kitchen. Sarah Mae got used to it yet?

GEORGE: Yeah. The chickens have too. It was a good idea to build two back doors, one right across from the other, 'cause it makes it cooler when she's cooking, but the chickens just run through like it was wide open spaces.

LAWRENCE *(laughs):* They better watch out. Just makes it easier for her to catch 'em.

SARAH MAE *(just as* LAWRENCE *says this she enters running, as if chasing chickens):* Come back here, you low-down dirty rascal. When I catch you, I'm gonna wring your neck!

LAWRENCE: Hey, Sarah Mae!

SARAH MAE *(whoops and slaps her thighs)*: Hey, Lawrence. When did yens get here?

LAWRENCE: Just now.

SARAH MAE: Well come and help me catch some of these chickens. I need a couple more fryers and a hen or two to roast.

LAWRENCE: My boys'll be along in a minute. They'll do that for you. 'Fact, they'd think it was fun. Come on over here.

SARAH MAE: All right. Where's Florence?

LAWRENCE: They're on the way up; had to stop and rest.

SARAH MAE *(whoops and slaps her thighs)*: Lawrence married Florence. That still tickles the tar out of me.

LAWRENCE: Me too. That's why I named my boys Joe and Bo, and my girl Zoe.

GEORGE: Yen's a regular poem.

LAWRENCE: Nah, I like it 'cause it sounds like a song.

SARAH MAE: You bring your fiddle?

LAWRENCE: Yep. Left it down in the barn waiting for the first couple to kick up the straw. How you been, Sis?

SARAH MAE: I been doing real good. 'Cept my feet been giving me a little trouble. I don't know what's wrong with 'em. They just pain me, you know, off and on.

LAWRENCE: Is that why you couldn't catch that old rooster just now?

SARAH MAE *(chuckles)*: Could be. I been complaining with 'em now a few months. Poultice don't help. I don't know what to do for 'em.

GEORGE *(he has been looking at her feet while she talks; now, he slowly drawls)*: Looks to me like you could take a little water to 'em.

(They all look for a moment at SARAH MAE's bare feet, which are crusty with dirt. SARAH MAE whoops and slaps her thighs, and they all laugh.)

SARAH MAE: Yep, you may be right.

(JESSIE enters from house, sweeping furiously. The other three begin coughing.)

GEORGE: Dang! It's a dust devil!

SARAH MAE: Jessie, stop! Jessie! Stop that this minute, child.

JESSIE: I'm just sweeping the yard like you told me.

SARAH MAE: Ain't you never swept a yard before? You have to mind the dust.

DOVEY *(enters from house, through the dust, coughing):* Jessie, what are you doing?

JESSIE: Trying to help Aunt Sarah Mae, Granny.

DOVEY: Well, you're making things worse. Land sakes, it's a good thing we don't have the tablecloths on yet.

SARAH MAE: Show her how to sprinkle the dirt down with a little water, Dovey.

DOVEY: Shore enough. Afore she sweeps the front yard.

JESSIE: Already done it.

DOVEY: Dog take it, that red dirt'll be drifting down below on Prudence's clean sheets. I seen she had them hanging out on the line.

SARAH MAE: Ah, don't fret about it. They ain't her clean wash. It's just her old signal sheets.

DOVEY: Oh. Well that's good. *(She and JESSIE move to the background, where she shows her how to dip her hand in a bucket and sprinkle water lightly over the yard. JESSIE can continue to sweep softly in the background, pause to listen sometimes, etc.)*

LAWRENCE: Signal sheets? What kind of signal?

GEORGE: To some fellers up at their still, up there on the bluff. She sees anybody that don't belong here regular, she warns them 'case it be the sheriff or revenuers. She sends a message by the way she hangs things on her clothesline.

LAWRENCE: For Pete's sake, that's as bad as Uncle Bruce hiding his moonshine in Mason jars buried in his flowerbed.

SARAH MAE: Yep. He was forever going out to pick a little bouquet.

LAWRENCE: Shucks, he'll always be a rebel.

DOVEY: God love 'im, what a heathen!

GEORGE: Yep, he's a lost cause. Lost as a bygone.

SARAH MAE: Don't say that.

GEORGE: Why?

SARAH MAE: 'Cause he's family.

GEORGE: Don't I know he's my own flesh and blood? I still say he'll never change.

SARAH MAE: Aw, he'll come around.

LAWRENCE: What makes you think so?

SARAH MAE: 'Cause family's more than just flesh and blood. Family's more about how close you are to somebody in the heart.

GEORGE: Uncle Bruce's heart is so stubborn he don't want to be close to nothing. I don't think even God could change it.

LAWRENCE: Maybe God's more concerned about changing our hearts than his'n.

SARAH MAE: Could be. I been pondering on him a good deal lately. Maybe we ain't never showed him enough sunshine, so he just looked for what he could find in his moonshine.

SAM *(enters):* Where's some moonshine?

SARAH MAE: You come to the wrong place. "Wine is a mocker, strong drink is raging, and whosoever is deceived thereby is not wise." Proverbs, chapter 20, verse 1.

SAM: I shore did come to the wrong place. I didn't know this was preaching. Howdy, George, Dovey. I passed your family a ways down, Lawrence. They're almost here. *(Studies* LAWRENCE *for a moment)* What you looking so *grave* about? You been in any more *grave* conditions lately? You been *coffin* any? *(Laughs)*

DOVEY: You hush up, Sam. You don't have to poke fun just 'cause you don't believe in miracles.

SAM: I believe in them, just not in my own family. Iff'n you quit butting in, that would be a miracle.

DOVEY: I'm talking about miracles where a body got raised from the dead.

GEORGE: Well, the body says he don't wanna talk about it.

ALICE *(enters):* Well lawzee me! Look who's here. Good to see you, Lawrence. Hey, Sam.

SAM: C'mere, Alice. They trying to say I don't believe in miracles.

ALICE: Well, you say you been born again. That's the biggest one I ever heered tell of.

(Everybody laughs.)

LAWRENCE: Let's ask Sam about that experience, Dovey. You been *born* lately, Sam? What did it feel like to be *born*?

SAM: I don't wanna talk about it.

LAWRENCE: Yeah, I figured.

SARAH MAE: Yens hush up now, making fun of holy things. Mind, this is our Maw's sideyard.

ALICE: Amen.

SAM: I don't see her listening nowhere.

ALICE: She's gonna come back and haint you iff'n you don't hush.

SAM: This might be her coming now.

(FLORENCE, JOE, BO, *and* ZOE *enter, exhausted. General welcomes. The kids sprawl on the ground.*)

DOVEY *(yelling back to house)*: Jim, bring your Aunt Florence a chair.

JIM *(yells)*: OK, Mama.

LAWRENCE *(because of* LAWRENCE's *"resurrection," there is a special tenderness between* FLORENCE *and him)*: You tuckered out, Sugar?

FLORENCE: Boy, am I glad you moved to Asheville before I met you!

LAWRENCE: Shucks, wouldn't I be worth the climb anyhow?

FLORENCE: Yes sir, you know you would.

(JIM *and* IRIS *enter with straight chairs.*)

JIM: Well, look here at all my uncles and aunts!

LAWRENCE *(looking carefully around)*: No, I don't see all of them. *(Crosses and takes chair)* C'mere and rest yourself, Florence.

FLORENCE *(as she sits)*: Why, thank you, Jim. *(To* LAWRENCE*)* Where *is* Uncle Carmel?

IRIS: He'll be along directly. Had a wedding in Sevierville today.

LAWRENCE: Don't say a word to him about it, Florence.

FLORENCE: How are you, Iris? *(To* LAWRENCE—*two conversations at once)* Can I hug him at least?

IRIS: Fine, thank you, ma'am. And you?

LAWRENCE: As long as you don't discuss it.

FLORENCE *(to* IRIS*)*: Very well.

LAWRENCE *(as if she had said "very well" to him)*: OK then.

DOVEY: Jessie! Come here and see your cousins.

LAWRENCE: Joe, you and Bo say hey to Jessie; then run and catch some chickens for dinner.

JOE: Yes, sir! Hey, Jessie.

BO: Hey, Jessie. Where are they, Daddy?

JESSIE: I saw Aunt Sarah Mae chasing them thataways somewheres.

JOE: Oh boy, let's go! (JOE *and* BO *run off.*)

SAM: What they saying down in Asheville about President Hoover, Lawrence?

LAWRENCE: Nothing good.

GEORGE: I read in the *Kansas City Star* that we ought to put him out.

FLORENCE: You get the *Star*, the newspaper, up here?

SAM: Only newspaper we do get. The rolling store comes down to the schoolhouse every couple weeks, and we can walk down and buy it.

SARAH MAE: Shoot, I wouldn't have much to paper over the cracks in the walls if we didn't get a newspaper. You wanna know what happened a few years back, just go read my wallpaper.

JESSIE: What's your name again?

ZOE: Zoe. I've got flowers on my wallpaper.

JESSIE: I got stripes. My name's Jessie.

ZOE: You got any brothers?

JESSIE: One. His name's Jamie. He's sitting over there in one of them trees.

DOVEY: He better mind he don't sit on a snake up there.

ZOE: Shoot, brothers are meaner than ary snake.

FLORENCE: Watch your speech, young lady.

JESSIE: Nah, Jamie ain't mean. He's just bashful. All these people scare him.

GEORGE: Don't blame him. We're a scary-looking bunch.

(ZOE *and* JESSIE *move US.*)

ALICE: Speak for yourself, George McCoy.

GEORGE: You think you're beautiful, Alice? Are you getting vain?

SAM: Shore she's vain—weathervane. Looks just like that rooster on top of the schoolhouse.

ALICE: I'll peck your eyes out too.

SARAH MAE: Yens leave Alice alone. She is a beauty.

ALICE: "Favor is deceitful and beauty is vain: but a woman that feareth the Lord, she shall be praised." Proverbs, chapter 31, verse 30. Holy Scripture.

SAM: I'm gonna put the fear of the Lord in your boy if he don't quit picking on my Ellen over there.

ALICE *(yelling offstage)*: Priestly! I'm gonna wear you out with that stick if you don't put it down.

(ELLEN *and* PRIESTLY *run by;* ALICE *grabs at the stick but misses.*)

ALICE: Wait'll your daddy gets back, boy!

(CARMEL *and* LINDY *are entering.* ELLEN *runs into* CARMEL *and grabs his legs;* PRIESTLY *stops short in front of him and lowers the stick.*)

CARMEL: What have we here?

PRIESTLY: A snake pole.

CARMEL: Sort of small for that, isn't it?

LINDY *(has a huckleberry box or whip made from tree bark; he goes past* CARMEL *and* PRIESTLY *to the others)*: Hey, everybody. Look what Uncle Carmel made me. Just like Daddy used to make.

CARMEL: You wouldn't lie to a preacher, would you, son?

PRIESTLY: No, sir.

LINDY: Is Daddy not here yet?

SARAH MAE: He's sitting in the house, Lindy. Kinda got a hitch in his getalong or something. Where's Connie and Susie?

LINDY *(laughs as he goes toward house)*: I don't think they'll ever come back up here, Aunt Sarah Mae. At least, not till the road comes all the way up and you get a bathroom.

SARAH MAE: Aw, we don't need either one.

(JIM *and* IRIS *exit with* LINDY, *miming conversation.*)

CARMEL: Do you know what the scripture says about lying, Priestly?

PRIESTLY: No, sir.

CARMEL: "All liars shall have their part in the lake which burneth with fire and brimstone: which is the second death" (Revelation 21:8).

PRIESTLY: What does "second death" mean?

CARMEL: Well, when somebody dies—(CARMEL *has spotted* LAWRENCE.) Never mind, son. *(With his eyes on* LAWRENCE, CARMEL *breaks the stick over his knee and goes to him.* Priestly *runs off;* Ellen *joins* Jessie *and* Zoe, *who are making necklaces from clover or daisies by slitting the stem of one and pulling another through until the blossom catches in the slit.*)

CARMEL: It's good to see you, brother.

LAWRENCE: It's real good to see you, brother. *(They hug.)* Where's Effie and Bernice?

CARMEL: Effie had to stay home and tend Bernice. She had her smallpox shot for school, and it made her real sick. What's all that commotion?

(Sounds offstage of people talking, laughing, walking, etc.)

GEORGE: Aw, that's just Talmadge and a passel of them coming back. They been down to the mineral spring.

(Enter TALMADGE, EVE, SHIRLEY, SILAS, UNCLE BRUCE, FRANKLIN, JOHN ED, DAISY *[these go DS] and* DEXTER, BENNY, DAN, *and* JUNE *[these go US]. General greetings.)*

UNCLE BRUCE: Law me! I gotta lay down here and take me a nap. *(Lies down and is asleep almost immediately.)*

ALICE: What took yens so long?

TALMADGE: We went by Blowing Cave. Some of the kids had never seen it.

DOVEY: You make it all the way, Eve?

EVE: Just barely.

DOVEY: I never could make it. It's too si-gogglin' on the hill.

SHIRLEY: You should feel it, Aunt Dovey. Seems like January wind blowing on you.

DOVEY: Better mind you don't cool off too quick in this heat. It could make you seize up.

DAISY NELL: My paw's gone over the mountain and seen the other end of the cave. It sucks air in on that side.

FRANKLIN: No it don't.

JOHN ED: Does too, Franklin. Ask our paw.

SARAH MAE: He's up to the house, John Ed.

JOHN ED: Well, ask Uncle George.

FRANKLIN: Uncle George, is that so?

GEORGE: Well now, in summer it does. In the winter that side blows out and our side sucks in. Ain't that right, Tadge?

TALMADGE: It just swaps ends with itself.

DEXTER: Huh, I've known some people like that.

DAISY NELL: Told you.

EVE: Is that the cave where Uncle Bruce used to have his still?

TALMADGE: Naw, that was the big caverns over near Grapevine Holler. Sam, remember that time we was walking home from school and found that place where the grapevines growed so thick they covered the trees over?

CARMEL: I do.

(*As often happens in a large group, two conversations are now going at once.*)

SARAH MAE: You ever been in them caverns, Eve?

SAM: Ah, Carmel, you was scared to climb up there.

CARMEL: That's right.

EVE: No, Talmadge won't take us over there. He's scared to go in under the ground.

SAM: You shoulda went. Ain't often you find vines so old and thick that they jump from tree to tree.

SARAH MAE: Well, it goes way-the-fool back under the ground. You just gotta carry you some good lanterns.

(PRIESTLY *reenters upstage with* ZELBERT. *They sit with* BENNY *and* DAN.)

TALMADGE: You could walk around on the top of the trees like it was a roof.

DOVEY: You have to hunker down through this little low hole for a piece, but then it opens up to a big old room like a courthouse or something, with halls commencing here, there, and yonder.

CARMEL: You almost fell through one time, Tadge.

DOVEY: Big creek back at the end of one of them. Just disappears under the mountain.

TALMADGE: Well, you had to watch where you stepped.

SARAH MAE: Purtiest things growing up out of the ground and down from the ceilings. Pointy things—like a bed of big spikes, 'cept they're slickery.

SAM: I liked to just lay up there and look at the clouds.

BENNY: They're going to start telling those old tales again.

SHIRLEY: Stag-mites or everwhat Teacher called them.

DAN: Let's go play Blind Man's Bluff.

EVE: I'd like to see that.

(ALL KIDS: *general agreement and excitement.*)

ZOE: That'll be kind of dangerous up here, won't it?

DAN: Why?

ZOE: Well, the blind man could walk off a real bluff.

BENNY: No, we have to watch him. If he gets in danger we yell, "Blacksnake!" and he knows to go another way.

PRIESTLY *(to* DEXTER*)*: You got ary handkerchief, Paw? (DEXTER *gives him a large handkerchief suitable for a blindfold.*) Zelbert, yens come on.

(ALL KIDS *run as far as possible to the side DR. They quickly choose* JOHN ED *to be "it" and blindfold him. He stands in the middle with his hands out while all the others place one hand on his, or one another's, creating a stack.*)

ZELBERT: John Ed, how many horses has your paw got?

JOHN ED: Two.

ZELBERT: What color are they?

JOHN ED: Black and gray.

ZELBERT: Crack away!

(ALL KIDS *exit running.*)

JOHN ED *(waits a few seconds and yells)*: Still waters! *(Waits a few seconds again and yells)* Moving waters! *(Listens to try to determine where they are; exits as if going to search for them)*

BO *(enters opposite; to* LAWRENCE*)*: Daddy, we caught six chickens. Joe's holding them in a tow sack.

SARAH MAE: Why, much obliged, Bo. Yens go take them to Irene in the kitchen and she'll show you how to wring their necks.

BO: Oh boy!

LAWRENCE: Then y'all can play with the rest of the kids.

DEXTER: Here, I'll go help with the chickens. *(He and* BO *exit.)*

PRUDENCE *(enters DL with her four daughters,* DAKOTA, WYOMING, VIRGINIA, NEBRASKA; *they carry two filled baskets)*: Hey, everybody. Sorry we're late. Had a little business to take care of.

SAM: Yeah, Prudence, we noticed on the way up. We seen you're *still* in business; *still* hanging out sheets. You been about four sheets to the wind, ain't you?

PRUDENCE: You should know. And I ain't in business. I just warn them when I see trouble coming. I don't want no deputies shooting it up around my house. Hey there, Eve. You remember my daughters? This here's Dakota, Wyoming, Virginia, and Nebraska.

EVE: It's good to see you again. What pretty girls.

SAM: Yeah, you girls just leave me in a *state*.

PRUDENCE: You oughta be in the moving pictures, Sam.

SAM: Why, thank you.

PRUDENCE: So nobody could hear your ijit jokes.

ALICE: Speaking of pretty girls, where's my Fern?

SARAH MAE: She's helping Irene in the kitchen.

ALICE: Just so she ain't off with John Ed. I swannee, sometimes I think they forget they're cousins.

FLORENCE *(to two of the girls):* Here, I'll take your baskets to the kitchen.

VIRGINIA: Oh, what a becoming dress. Did you make it yourself?

FLORENCE: Sure did.

TALMADGE: You got a sewing machine, Florence?

FLORENCE: Yes, I do.

TALMADGE: That's good. That's real good. My maw never had one.

VIRGINIA: I want me a dress made off the pattern, Mama. From those pretty flowerdy feedsacks you got.

WYOMING: Not me. I want mine out of dotted swiss. Can we use your pattern, Aunt Florence?

FLORENCE: Well, if I can find some way to get it over here from Asheville.

(Men's voices approaching offstage, singing "She'll be Coming 'Round the Mountain.")

GEORGE: Yonder comes Othey and his boys.

(OTHEY, GROVER, DELBERT, BILLY ROY enter UL, still singing. EULABELLE enters behind them. BESSIE JEAN is clinging to her skirt and does so throughout. The whole crowd can join them in one last verse. UNCLE BRUCE wakes and stands. FLORENCE exits to kitchen with baskets.)

DOVEY: That was fine, boys, mighty fine.

(They introduce themselves and bow, one at a time.)

OTHEY: The Singing McCoys. I'm Othey.

GROVER: I'm Grover.

DELBERT: I'm Delbert.

BILLY ROY: I'm Billy Roy.

GEORGE: That was kind of you, Eulabelle, to bear Othey your own little quartet.

EULABELLE: Why, thank you, George. I'm glad somebody remembers I had something to do with it.

TALMADGE: Y'all know any Chuck Wagon Gang?

(The quartet sings "Kneel at the Cross" or "Just a Little Talk with Jesus" or "On the Jericho Road.")

SARAH MAE: Purt near heavenly, boys. Go on up to the kitchen if you will and sing one for them that's cooking.

CARMEL: Go sing for your supper, Old Dan Tucker.

(OTHEY and the three boys exit as JIM, IRIS, LINDY, and FLORENCE reenter with something for the tables.)

LAWRENCE: I seen you tapping your foot over there, Uncle Bruce.

UNCLE BRUCE: 'Course I was. 'Cause I like good music. Pleasures me right smart.

SAM: You ain't done got religion?

UNCLE BRUCE: You know better than that. And don't be asking it anymore. I don't have to listen to you.

JIM: Why you always been so stubborn about becoming a Christian, Uncle Bruce?

UNCLE BRUCE: Because of some Christians I know.

IRIS: That don't seem like a very good reason.

UNCLE BRUCE: Well, it's the same reason I fought on the Yankees' side of the War.

LINDY *(exclamation):* On the Yankees' side?

GEORGE *(to* UNCLE BRUCE*):* Hush up, traitor! We don't speak about such as that.

JIM: Why did you do that?

UNCLE BRUCE: For spite. 'Cause the consarned rebels come by my house wanting me to sign up, and I said, "Man, my wife just had our first little baby. I can't go off to no war. Ain't nobody around close to look after her or keep her up. I can't leave her right now. I'll come later if you still need me."

LINDY: What happened?

UNCLE BRUCE: Dog take it if they didn't conscript me in anyway. You think I'd fight for anybody that would be so disrespectful? No sir, I would not. Just because they tried to force me to join them, they made me so mad that I turned against them to the other side. Guess I showed them whether they could force me to do anything or not.

NEBRASKA: How did you do that?

UNCLE BRUCE: It wasn't long before we camped real close to a Union camp. In the middle of the night I sneaked off and told them I wanted to switch to their side. *(Chuckles)* Showed them who they could draft and who they couldn't.

GEORGE: Turncoat.

UNCLE BRUCE: Served them right.

LINDY: Well, I don't know if I can call you Great Uncle Bruce anymore. I just might have to leave the "great" off.

IRIS *(to* UNCLE BRUCE*)*: I don't see a thing in the world that's got to do with Christians.

UNCLE BRUCE: 'Cause they're always coming around trying to force me to be one. Just keep on preaching at me; never let up. I disremember when my mind got so feeble that somebody else had to make it up for me. Makes me dig my heels in even harder.

DAKOTA: You trying to say you done gone over to the devil's side?

UNCLE BRUCE: No, not exactly. Sometimes it just seems better to sorta straddle the fence.

ALICE: If you ain't on the Lord's side, you're on the devil's. They ain't no sitting in between.

UNCLE BRUCE: You see what I tell you? They never let up. I'm the oldest man around these parts, and they still try to tell me what to do. Let 'em, they'll tell me how to wear my overalls.

PRUDENCE: Well hitch up your galluses, 'cause my girls are gonna sing a gospel song too.

(VIRGINIA, WYOMING, DAKOTA, *and* NEBRASKA *sing; then perhaps the male quartet has returned and joins them in another song. After that,* OTHEY *remains and the three boys and four girls sit far upstage so they are effectively out of the action.)*

UNCLE BRUCE: That was real good, yens. Yep, music does an old man's heart good.

JIM: But them was church songs, Uncle Bruce.

UNCLE BRUCE: I know that! You trying to make fun of me, boy? I been in a church once't or twice't in my life.

JIM: Did you and Great Aunt Sadie go when your boys was little?

UNCLE BRUCE: We let the boys go, but she stayed home with me.

IRIS: Sadie not ever get religion either?

UNCLE BRUCE: I don't rightly know. None of us ever talked about it.

FLORENCE: You got a wife and two boys already passed on and you don't know if they're saved or not?

UNCLE BRUCE: I didn't say that now. Willie was too young when he died, but me and Sadie went to see Bradley baptized. We just didn't talk about it, you know, for ourselves.

FLORENCE: Why not?

UNCLE BRUCE: I reckon 'cause she heered me fuss so much about folk trying to sway me into being a Christian. Maybe I made too much of a fuss about it. Maybe if people woulda leave me be I would've hushed up and she might have decided . . . but they just stayed on me like flies on a watermelon.

JIM: Were they really that bad, or did you just blow it up in your mind?

UNCLE BRUCE: I swear if Jed didn't get revived up one night and come and sing "Almost Persuaded" under my window just for meanness. Picking on me got to be a joke—to everybody but me. But Sadie, she knowed what kind of man I was. She knowed I'd do to wade the river with. 'Sides, I thought I'd be dead and buried first. But here I am, last of all. It ain't fair.

PRUDENCE: I know it ain't been easy to live alone.

UNCLE BRUCE: No, it gives you a lot of time to sit and wonder about things. Sometimes I think the wondering is the worst part.

SARAH MAE: You never said nothing about that, Uncle Bruce. I didn't know you was worried—

(ZELBERT *and* DAISY NELL *run in.*)

DAISY NELL: Uncle George, Cousin Silas is afixin' to carve on your burying tree.

ZELBERT: He won't pay us no mind.

GEORGE: Lord-a-mercy! *(Calls to offstage)* Silas! Get away from that tree!

TALMADGE: Silas! I'll tan your hide, boy. Get over here with that knife. *(Holds hand out for knife)*

SILAS *(enters with SHIRLEY and FRANKLIN)*: We was just gonna carve our initials in a tree, like you said you used to. *(Surrenders knife to TALMADGE)*

GEORGE: Not in that tree, you ain't. That there is a sacred tree.

SHIRLEY: It is?

GEORGE: Yep.

ZELBERT: Told you; told you; now I get to hold you! *(Grabs SHIRLEY by the wrists, but she kicks him on the shin or behind his knees and he releases her.)*

FRANKLIN: How can you tell?

GEORGE: Didn't you hear it sing? *(SILAS and SHIRLEY exchange looks.)* Yeah, when the wind blows through the limbs it sings hymns. *(If desired he can hum the first line or two of an old funeral song.)* That's my burying tree.

SHIRLEY: Your what tree?

GEORGE: Burying.

SILAS: I ain't never heard tell of such.

TALMADGE: Silas, you know what burying somebody means.

SILAS: Not in a tree, I don't.

TALMADGE: No son, when the time comes they'll cut it down and make his box.

GEORGE: Been watching it grow for years now. Picked it out myself. Straight and true. Keep all the kudzu away from it; sapsuckers too. It's 'bout big enough now.

EVE: And you call us kin from the East peculiar?

GEORGE: Ain't peculiar; it's just being prepared. Never know when you'll go, do you, Lawrence? *(No answer)* Jesus said that we didn't know when He'd come; it would be just as sudden as lightning.

EVE: What if lightning strikes your tree?

(Laughter)

EULABELLE: George is as strange as Uncle Jed. He's had his coffin made and a'settin' in his hallway for years.

SHIRLEY: Mama, is these people really our uncles?

EULABELLE: Yep. Got up and laid in it for good measure.

JIM: The devil he did!

EULABELLE: No, it warn't. It was Uncle Jed hisself.

OTHEY: Now that's what I call getting too much pre-blasted-pared.

GEORGE: Shoot, no. Just save your kin some trouble. Jed's got a box; I'm getting a box; Lawrence had a box. Did you save your box after you got back, Lawrence?

IRIS: Got back from where?

SAM: He ain't gonna talk about it. You just as well put a milk bucket under a bull.

CARMEL: No, he didn't save it. He smashed it to smithereens and burned it for firewood.

(SARAH MAE *slaps her thighs and whoops.*)

DOVEY: "Death is swallowed up in victory. O death, where is thy sting? O grave, where is thy victory?" (1 Corinthians 15:54*b*-55).

ALICE: I miss Maw.

BESSIE JEAN: You believe in Maw and Paw?

SARAH MAE: I wish I had some of her green beans.

TALMADGE: How many messes of beans you reckon she put up in her lifetime?

BESSIE JEAN: Thirty, 40.

SAM: I wish Maw and Paw could be here. I think they'd be purt near proud.

BESSIE JEAN: You believe in Maw and Paw?

SHIRLEY: Why does she keep saying that?

EULABELLE: Ah, she gets things a mite addled. She means, "You believe in Santy Claus?" *(Some kids laugh)* Shush now!

ALICE: Yeah, I think Maw and Paw did a good job. I know we got our faults, but we ain't like some families that act like they ain't got no raisings at all.

TALMADGE: I reckon so. We ain't got no outlaws, no robbers.

(*Everyone reflects silently for a couple beats; then three responses are slowly drawled, building on each other.*)

PRUDENCE: Othey robs the beehives.

SARAH MAE: Lawrence robbed the grave.

SAM: Uncle Mitchell robbed the cradle!

(Laughter)

EVE: What? What's he talking about?

DOVEY: Our Uncle Mitchell on our mama's side used to be real fond of a little neighbor girl. They would all be sitting on the porch visiting, and he would always rock her to sleep. Purty thing—with fair skin and long yellow curls. He was crazy about her. He used to rock her and say, "You sweet little gal, I'm gonna marry you someday."

SAM: And he did!

EVE: My stars! How long did he wait?

DOVEY: She must have been . . . what would you say, Eulabelle?

EULABELLE: About 13 or 14 year old.

BESSIE JEAN: Thirty, 40.

IRIS: Where are they now?

EULABELLE: He's dead. She soon married the feller that watched the fire tower and they moved to Waynesville. I wonder about her sometimes.

EVE: How many times was Uncle Mitchell married?

DOVEY: Just the once.

BESSIE JEAN: 'Bout 30, 40.

SILAS: Why does she keep saying "30, 40"?

EULABELLE: Well, those are the only numbers she knows.

FRANKLIN: Ah, I don't believe that. What's her name?

EULABELLE: Bessie Jean.

FRANKLIN: Hey, Bessie Jean.

BESSIE JEAN: Hey, Bessie Jean.

FRANKLIN: How old are you?

BESSIE JEAN *(holding up two fingers)*: a-b-c-d *(with strong emphasis on "c")*, 30, 40.

(ALL KIDS *laugh.*)

EULABELLE: No, no, musn't laugh. We don't laugh at her.

SILAS: Why not? She's funny.

DOVEY: 'Cause she's family, Son, and she don't know no better. Families stick up for each other.

SARAH MAE: Don't forget that, Silas. Don't none of yens forget it. Family is something to watch over no matter what. Family's like a safe hiding place—like when whoever's "It" hollers, "Home Free!" Family's where you ought to always be loved and accepted just like you are.

UNCLE BRUCE: Humph.

ALICE: That's the way the Lord accepts us.

GEORGE: Amen.

OTHEY: Amen. Sing it, boys.

(Quartet starts "Just As I Am." Most of the crowd joins in. Some of the kids can wander back in US during the song if you wish.)

UNCLE BRUCE: Well, yens was really getting into that song. Does that mean yens is prepared to accept me just as I am, Christian or not?

DOVEY: Shore does, Uncle Bruce.

UNCLE BRUCE: You know, I never thought about the words to that song much before today. But that's a gen-u-wine decent way to act—love and accept folk no matter how they are. The way Jesus' people oughta act, too, I figure.

EULABELLE: Shore it is.

UNCLE BRUCE: Well, is yens a'saying your faith's gonna make you act that way?

(It is evident from everyone's looks and body positions that they are daring to hope that UNCLE BRUCE is almost ready to make a decision to become a Christian. They lean closer and closer toward him, almost breathless, afraid to break the spell.)

OTHEY: Yep, I reckon that's what we're saying.

UNCLE BRUCE: Well, I'm glad to know it! Now maybe you'll leave me alone!

(Everyone falls back; try for a comic effect.)

SARAH MAE: Oh, I don't know about that. When you love a body the last thing you want to do is leave them alone.

CARMEL: We don't want to be alone. That's why we have these family reunions.

UNCLE BRUCE: Dad-blamedest family I know!

SARAH MAE: Ain't we though? *(Whoops and slaps her thighs)* Still, we *is* family.

GEORGE: We've claimed you no matter how you lived, and we'll bury you no matter how you die.

DAISY NELL: Have you got a coffin too?

UNCLE BRUCE: No, but I sure as blazes got a family.

ALICE: Family's probably the most important thing you got.

ZELBERT: Daddy said God's the most important thing.

TALMADGE: Why, you're righter than rain, Zelbert. But God's the one who thought of families. You look in your Bible and see. That's how He planned for us to live—in little small groups. A body can go out and about, and lots of times meet up with bullies and scalawags. He can come on trouble and be treated poorly. He can be just as disappointed as a thunderhead that never rains, and he can work like a plow horse with a harness that's too tight. Somehow he can survive through it all if he knows he's got a family, that if he knocks on the door they're gonna say, "Come on in here, boy. You one of us."

DOVEY: God didn't just sling things He made out into the world like hayseed. Everything's got a place where it belongs.

GEORGE: Yeah, we need a place where everybody's familiar, so we don't all be wandering around in a world of strangers like mongrel dogs.

PRUDENCE: I think God wants us to have a cozy, close place where we got somebody that tries to understand us. Somewhere that we feel loved. Shoot, that's even how He starts new families—when two people fall in love and get married.

SAM: Boy, howdy! That's how our family growed to all these here and more besides. Who even knows how many?

BESSIE JEAN: Thirty, 40.

SAM: So many I can't cipher it out.

ALICE: And some of us is harder to love than others.

SARAH MAE: Well of course. Real jewels cost more than glass beads. And they take longer to form. And to cut and polish too.

ZELBERT: Pee Wee Barrett ain't got no family.

UNCLE BRUCE: Yeah, poor old Pee Wee's just a woods colt. Don't know who his daddy is; mama's dead.

DOVEY: Well, Zelbert, sometimes people are alone for one reason or another.

EVE: Seems like to me when Jesus walked this earth He went looking for folk that had sort of got put out of their place.

GEORGE: Yep, and I'd wager that's what He wants us to do too. Find them and include them in our family.

DOVEY: Yeah, we try to practice that. We've always invited Pee Wee to our dinners. He's on the back porch now helping shuck roas'in ears.

SARAH MAE: And if you ponder on it—you know, God practices what He preaches. He's got Him a family too, a big old family.

SHIRLEY: That's everybody in the whole world!

SARAH MAE: Well no, Honey. It's everybody that asks to be in His family. You're a preacher, Carmel. Tell her.

CARMEL: Well, let's see now. Did you hear Great Uncle Bruce talking about being forced to fight in the war? Now then, did you know there was once a big war in heaven? *(Comments of disbelief from some adults and all children)* Oh, yes. The angels raised a thunder in heaven worse than if Auger Rock up and broke loose and tumbled down the mountain on top of us. The trouble was, God created all the angels and placed them in heaven to serve Him. To fight on His side, so to speak. Well, some of them got mad, like Uncle Bruce did, because they didn't have a say-so in the matter. One of them said he was going to be greater than God, and a bunch of the angels went over to his side. I guess you know that was Satan, the devil. Of course, God couldn't stand for that, so there was a terrible ruckus and God had to kick about a third of the angels out of heaven. And they've been causing all of us nothing but mischief ever since. Must have broken God's heart. Anyway, I think He must have decided that anybody who gets into heaven now is there because he wants to be—a body that makes his own choice and asks to become a member of God's family. If you want to be on God's side, He wants you to prove it by telling Him and telling other people. Can't say that I blame Him. You can live with God if you want, or you can live with the devil if you want. It's pretty simple, really.

PRUDENCE: Them that choose God will all live together someday in heaven in one big, everlasting family.

DOVEY: Some of our kin already there.

SHIRLEY: Really?

SILAS: Wonder what they're doing?

CARMEL: Well, I reckon they're having a big time.

GEORGE: All of us will sure 'nuff go see someday.

EULABELLE: *Some* of us might not.

DOVEY: Some of us might go sooner than we expected.

ALICE: Especially the ornery ones.

EULABELLE: The stubborn.

OTHEY: The ones that can't tell "Come 'ere" from "Sic 'em."

UNCLE BRUCE: Some of us might not care if we go or not.

TALMADGE: I reckon they're all waiting on us right now.

SARAH MAE: I reckon they're up there saying, "It's getting late."

EULABELLE: Real late.

ALICE: Maybe too late for comfort.

UNCLE BRUCE: Too late to change anything.

SAM: It's never too late on this earth, Uncle Bruce. I know that.

UNCLE BRUCE: You don't know nothing! I don't neither! Sadie—I didn't even get to talk to her. Who knows what happened to her? She just . . . went.

(Pause)

GEORGE: I miss them: Granny, Maw, Paw.

SARAH MAE: Janie and her twins.

CARMEL: Uncle Bruce's Sadie.

DOVEY: It will be so good when we can all be together again.

UNCLE BRUCE: Well, what are you all looking at me for?

SARAH MAE: I 'spect that's what the song means—will the circle be unbroken? Will everybody be there?

UNCLE BRUCE: You don't know nothing. There might not even be a heaven.

SARAH MAE: Yes there is!

UNCLE BRUCE: Besides, my Sadie might not even be there!

(Long pause. Total silence onstage.)

LAWRENCE: She's there.

(Everybody stares at LAWRENCE. This is the first word he's ever uttered about his "death." CARMEL goes to him and touches his shoulder or arm; they exchange a long look. Someone begins to sing "Will the Circle Be Unbroken?" The whole family joins the singing, forming a circle and holding hands, except for UNCLE BRUCE. LAWRENCE holds out one hand to UNCLE BRUCE, who still hesitates. CARMEL leaves the circle, goes to UNCLE BRUCE, puts his arm around him, and leads him to take LAWRENCE's hand. CARMEL takes his other hand and completes the circle as the song continues joyfully.)

APPENDIX

Family Tree

WILL McCOY (Paw)—1855-1908
married MACIE DOCKERY (Maw)—1862-1905
remarried BIRDIE CODY in 1905; both WILL and BIRDIE died of typhoid in 1908

Children of WILL and MACIE

SARAH MAE McCOY, born 1879. Never married. Lives in old homeplace.

JANIE McCOY BUSH—1880-95. Married ISAAC BUSH. No children (stillborn twins).

BART McCOY, born 1883. Widower of OLLIE. Lives in mountains.
Children: LINDY, married to CONNIE. Live in Charlotte, North Carolina.
Child: SUSIE
JOHN ED
MARY LOU
ZELBERT
DAISY NELL

GEORGE McCOY, born 1886. Never married. Lives in old homeplace.

DOVEY McCOY LEE, born 1888. Widow of JAMES LEE. Lives in mountains.
Child: JIM, married to IRIS. Live in Seviereville.
Children:
JESSIE
JAMIE

ALICE McCOY GOLIGHTLY, born 1888. Married to DEXTER. Live in mountains.
Children:
PRIESTLY
FERN

SAM McCOY, born 1891. Married to IRENE. Live in mountains.
Children:
BENNY
ELLEN
DAN
ZACK

TALMADGE McCOY, born 1893. Married to EVE. Live in Spartanburg, South Carolina.
Children:
SILAS
JUNE
SHIRLEY
FRANKLIN

CARMEL McCOY, 1895—1933. Married to EFFIE. Lived in Newport, Tennessee.
Child: BERNICE

LAWRENCE McCOY, born 1897. Married to FLORENCE. Live in Asheville, North Carolina.
Children:
JOE
ZOE
BO

PRUDENCE PRATT, born 1894. Widow of CARL. (Stepsister—child of BIRDIE CODY.) Lives in mountains.
Children:
DAKOTA
VIRGINIA
WYOMING
NEBRASKA

UNCLE JED McCOY, born 1874. Brother of WILL. Married to Queen Victoria. Lives in mountains, but he travels.
Child: OTHEY, married to EULABELLE.
Children:
GROVER
BESSIE JEAN
DELBERT
ELIZABETH
BILLY ROY

UNCLE BRUCE DOCKERY, born 1843. MACIE'S brother. Widower of SADIE. Lives in mountains.

Some Suggested Songs

From Albert E. Brumley's *Olde Time Camp Meetin' Songs*, 345 W. Highway 54, Camdenton, MO 65020.
- "Church in the Wildwood"
- "I'll Fly Away"
- "Will the Circle Be Unbroken?"
- "O Why Not Tonight"
- "Where We'll Never Grow Old"
- "Farther Along"
- "This World Is Not My Home"
- "Never Alone"
- "Unclouded Day"
- "Where the Soul Never Dies"
- "Hold to God's Unchanging Hand"
- "Stand by Me"
- "Precious Memories"
- "Will There Be Any Stars in My Crown?"

The following in most old hymnals:
- "Safe in the Arms of Jesus"
- "In the Sweet By and By"
- "Let Him In"
- "Stepping in the Light"
- "Why Do You Wait?"
- "Look and Live"
- "When I Can Read My Title Clear"

You might also include some nonreligious songs, especially ballads like "Barbara Allen" and "Billy Boy."

Glossary

Requires less mouth movement:

afore	before	ijit	idiot
agin	again	jist	just
ain't	are not	lack	like
argy	argue	mawl	mall
arn	iron	Moundy	Monday
Arsh	Irish	narrer	narrow
awl	all	piller	pillow
back'urds	backwards	pneumony	pneumonia
Caroliny	Carolina	pore	poor
cawfee	coffee	presydent	president
cheer	chair	properdy	property
deppidy	deputy	purty	pretty
dreckly	directly	reglar	regular
edgycation	education	reench	wrench
et	ate	ruther	rather
ever	every	shore	sure
everbody	everybody	sitchiation	situation
everwhur	everywhere	sich	such
extry	extra	summers	somewhere
famly	family	sump'un	something
far	fire	thanky	thank you
feller	fellow	they wuz	there was
finely	finally	tolable	tolerable
figger	figure	torj	towards
folk	folks	t'reckly	directly
haint	haunt (a ghost)	wont	want
hep	help	widder	widow
idy	idea	winder	window
idn't	isn't	wuhdn't	wasn't or wouldn't
		wuz	was

year	years
ye	you
yestudy	yesterday

Requires less words:

a'tall	at all
being's	it being that
doanchee	don't you
dunno	don't know
evertime	every time
frunchard	front yard
gonna	going to
Jeet?	Did you eat?
Jever?	Did you ever?
Ju have?	Did you have?
kindly	kind of
oughter	ought to
racheer	right here
sorta	sort of
so's	so as or so
'spect	expect or suspect
summers	somewhere
t'	to
t'ain't	it is not
thataway	in that way or that way
tolju	I told you
t'other	the other
usta	used to
warn't	was not
whatchew or whatcha	what are you
woodju	would you
woulda	would have
yens	you ones, all of you: equal to y'all
yont	do you want
you	you are
young'uns	young ones

Some drawn out words:

Bee-ul	Bill
beh-ud	bed
daintz	dance
me-un	men
own	on
sho-ur	sure
ske-ur	scare
teh-ul	tell
yeh-us	yes

Some tenses and pronouns:

clumb	climbed
fit	fought
hisself	himself
knowed	knew or known
ruint	ruined
seed	saw or seen
theirselves	themselves
yer	your
yorn	yours
hern	hers
his'n	his

Idioms:

allows	states the conclusion that or declares
ary/nary	Approximately the same meaning as "any" and "none" "Have you got ary coat?" "There was nary a star in the sky."
beg to differ	disagrees with
biggety	pompous

botherment	annoyance	misdoubt	don't believe
brogans	heavy lace-up shoes	moonin'	love sick
Chucky Jack	Revolutionary War hero John Sevier, for whom Sevier County was named	nary	not any
		no you ain't	term of astonishment
		passel	large amount
		peak-ed	pale
disremember	don't remember or recall incorrectly	peench	pinch
		peppering down	hard rain, about one-half of a gulley-washer or Toad-strangler
do to wade the river with	can be trusted		
Dog take it	exclamation of aggravation		
		plumb	completely
earbobs	earrings	poke	bag
eh law	exclamation or term of consternation	po-lice	police
		purt near	almost
everwhat	whatever	raisings	upbringing
fur	far	right smart	a considerable quantity
flowerdy	flowered pattern	roasineers	roasting ears of corn
foolishment	foolishness	shut my mouth or shut your mouth	astonishment or "Isn't it the truth?"
galls	irritates		
git shet uv	get shut (rid) of		
hit	it		
holt	hold		
iffen	if	set	sit
in shurns	insurance	slickery	slick
knob	large high hill, rounded but steep, usually with no trees	so's	so
		teejus	tedious
		tetched in the head	crazy
ketch in my git-along	ache; stiffness	thangs	things
law me or lawzee me	exclamation	tight as Dick's hatband	extremely tight
like fightin' far	as if fighting fire: fast and vigorous	tote	carry
		whoop and a holler	the distance away that those sounds will carry
lit in on	attacked		
looky here!	exclamation		
might nigh	almost		

PERFORMANCE LICENSING AGREEMENT

Lillenas Drama Resources
Performance Licensing
P.O. Box 419527, Kansas City, MO 64141

Name _____

Organization _____

Address _____

City _____ State _____ ZIP _____

Play _____ **SARAH MAE AND HER KINFOLK** by Gail Blanton _____

Number of performances intended _____

Approximate dates _____

Amount remitted* $ _____

Mail to Lillenas at the address above.

Order performance copies of this script from your local bookstore or directly from the publisher.

*$25.00 for the first performance; $15.00 each subsequent performance